Autonomous Colleges in the Twenty-first Century

The contents of the book have the approval of the Chairperson, UGC and were commissioned by the Secretary, UGC

Autonomous Colleges in the Twenty-first Century

R P Singh
Editor

Originals
(an imprint of Low Price Publications)
Delhi-110052

Distributed By
D.K. Publishers Distributors (P) Ltd.
4834/24, Ansari Road, Darya Ganj,
New Delhi-110002
Phones: 3278584, 3278368, 3261465,
e-mail: dkpd@del3.vsnl.net.in
visit us at: www.dkpd.com

First Published 2001
ISBN 81-7536-262-6

Published By
Originals
(an imprint of Low Price Publications)
A-6, Nimri Commercial Centre,
Near Ashok Vihar Phase-IV,
Delhi-110052
Phones: 7401672, 7452453
e-mail: lpp@nde.vsnl.net.in
visit us at: www.lppindia.com

Printed At:
D K Fine Art Press P Ltd.
Delhi-110052

Contents

PREFACE

Considering that higher education is in a state of flux across the world, the tertiary system in India cannot remain immune from these upheavals. Three types of changes are evident in the area. The first one pertains to financing i.e. how much money is available for it and who are going to be its providers. The second one deals with education interfacing market forces, which means whether or not the degree holders of the tertiary system have potential skills and knowledge worth their salaries. And the third one tries to decide about the exact role of high-tech both in the curricula as well as a means of better, efficient and inexpensive mode of instruction. In all these three areas the existing system has shown signs of some activity verging on nervousness. But unfortunately, the responses to the emerging challenges are neither well co-ordinated nor efficient. The problem seems to be that the apex system has not grasped the seriousness of the malaise.

In order to make a highly regimented and structured system develop quick reflexes perhaps the caution one ought to take is to avoid tinkering with the functioning of the system. Instead, one should try to give it a totally new direction. It may not be easy to change the universities so much as it is easier to deal with the colleges. Firstly, they serve almost all sections of our society for a variety of reasons. Secondly, they are almost ubiquitous in their presence. Being close to the ground reality they can develop quick reflexes much better than the universities can because of the nature of their statutory requirements. Also, except in certain routine academic matters the colleges in India function as independent units. They have their management mechanisms and full academic staffs. They have their separate buildings and until recently different pay structures as well. Already there is a scheme operating to make these institutions autonomous. We may also acknowledge here that we are the only country in the world where the colleges as a system are older than the universities by almost a century. The roots of the colleges in the system of higher education are thus deeper and closer to the ground than those of the universities.

It is possible to free these colleges from the regimentation of universities and develop them as easy and better-managed institutions with instant reflexes. For this end in view let us recount what exactly has happened under the existing scheme. So far the number of such colleges is not more than 140. For the approval of their courses of study they have, in spite of their autonomy, to depend on the universities for approval. The universities conduct their examinations and announce the results of these colleges along with those of their own. In most cases the colleges are not free to change their fee structure either. For starting new courses they are dependent on the universities and follow strictly the academic calendars as fixed by the universities. For functioning as market-oriented commercial units they do not have the necessary authority or approval. Consequently, we have lot many coaching centers which attract college teachers to earn on the sly at the cost of teaching better and efficiently in their institutions. It is therefore very doubtful that they are in any sense autonomous. In the case of government colleges the teachers can be transferred as a policy prerogative of the bureaucrats. This is an additional problem of the government colleges. It is almost common knowledge that in the departmental structure it is always possible to transfer the inconvenient staff of one college to another. In the process both the good and the bad suffer almost equally.

From this scenario which is neither very promising nor worth continuing we should move on to a model which is both logical and workable. The ideal autonomous college is the one, which adopts a cafeteria approach to its clientele's demands. It does not offer a fixed menu and also does not say either "take this" or "leave". In fact, if we ever had a malleable structure like this one there would be no need for what we call "coaching institutes" and the type of ill-suited majority of students who are difficult to accommodate in the academic society. The number of fixed time- frame courses that the universities normally offer and force down the throats of the unwilling and recalcitrants has shown their adverse impact all around us. Look at the number of courses the American colleges can offer and the type of freedom college teachers have to start their individual courses of study and look at the way our colleges offer their fare and the type of freedom our college teachers have. If only we could see the difference between the two we would soon realize why the American Community Colleges are so different from our Autonomous Colleges which they were supposed to replicate in terms of both vibrancy and variety. If the community colleges can offer more than 20,000 courses of study ranging in terms of time frame from two weeks to five years, there is no reason why our institutions can not do so. If the community colleges raise their revenue by offering short term, fee-paying courses on public demand, the Indian market is fairly well developed to offer similar lucrative responses to these academic overtures. The first fall out if we were ever to do what I am proposing we do and that too immediately will be the sounding of the death-knell to the private coaching institutes. For once the students will have proper classes and qualified, competent teachers and the other infrastructure facilities, also, the dubiousness of the some in existence will also evaporate. When put in the hands of imaginative staff a few of these colleges could make numerous companies dealing with e-education course run for their money.

There are a variety of reasons why the Indian colleges are not very enthused about the proposal of autonomous colleges? Firstly, they have no past experience of having ever performed jobs that they must undertake now. They have no idea how individuals can take major decisions like offering a new course of study or trying to match their wits with the market forces and succeed. They have no system in place to evaluate, examine or process a market demand. In fact the Indian system has been so isolated and aloof from the market that even the courses which they currently offer for market consumption or on market demand are mainly theoretical and generally vacuous in nature. Secondly, they have no experience of evaluating answerbooks in public knowledge and face the consequences of their action. Thirdly, living in the security of both anonymity and routine a face- to- face confrontation with the reality is not a welcome proposal. To be always looking out for an emergent social requirement cannot be easily learnt. Thus far we are known by our designations and not by our real worth and the ability to face up to the challenges. The new experience being proposed would therefore not go down well with the majority. The scheme in existence is only a pallid version of the real requirement. People have a vague idea that the time is coming in near future when to think of tenure positions will soon become a thing for the past. The challenges that the high-tech poses scare the older staffs stiff with fear. They therefore wish to delay the eventuality.

Today by planning we mean only a budgetary commitment. In this case however the commitment has to move in the nature of realizing a dream and determined action. The dream is that the Indian system of education should become both internally as well as externally competitive. Internal competition should be directed against the universities in the sense that the courses offered at the college level should in no case be considered inferior to the best made available by the universities and at the same time the immediate needs of the business or society may not be overlooked. If a professional college, which is offering, say a degree or diploma in engineering what is the harm if during academic holidays or when the building is unoccupied short-tem refresher courses or paid workshops can be run. The idea is that the college building is a public property. Keeping it unoccupied for any length of time is an economic waste. In the context of the former the duration of the courses and the level of instruction should be comparable and competitive. And with regard to the latter these colleges should be so flexible and nubile that a single need of the either business or the community should never be allowed to go unattended by them. The idea is that these autonomous colleges should not be forced to follow an inflexible and lengthy regimen when they are in need of urgent change. One should never forget the reality that markets are fickle and the customer trendy. Delays act as spoil sport in the process. When a change in the curricula or in the duration of the new courses of study is desired change should be possible. No one would want that precautions should be thrown to the winds. Or, the market itself should move into the colleges. One needs to give the process of change due thought and a suitable mechanism has to be evolved for co-operation and co-ordination between the two systems— the academic and the market or industry. Already a few universities have evolved mechanisms but these require wide publicity.

What I have in mind are the Community Colleges of the United States of America as well as the professional colleges like those of engineering, medicine or agriculture that we already have. With the existing monoliths and moribund systems like the ones we already have we can not expect much. It is not possible without an independent body to take care of these concerns. Therefore I recommend that the autonomous colleges should be taken out of the purview of the UGC and handed over to an elected body of suitable number of working principals in each State. A small number of their representatives through election may constitute their Apex body to negotiate or have dialogue with different government bodies. In both cases the term of the governing body members will be fixed and no re-election of the candidate to any body should be possible. This loosely federated arrangement may be better able to advise, than the existing government bodies.

It is very appropriate to recall the functioning of colleges in India before the universities came into existence. It would also be interesting to think of the reasons why Universities were set up here in the first place. From the beginning it was to control the system that schemes and statutes were made and not to allow them to function as the academics thought it fit to run. The idea is not to go back in history or seek any inspiration from the past practices. All that I wish to emphasize is that colleges have been run without being overseen by the universities. And if this is so, then why do we need a body like the University Grants Commission with highly structured and hierarchy ridden mechanism to come and unnecessary interfere with a system it has neither the means nor imagination to advise or provide any leadership whatsoever. Money is needed but the leadership is even more essential. Even with the best of the intentions the UGC has already lost numerous opportunities in several other areas as well, therefore to think that the leviathan will stand up and coordinate its own limbs and brain is by itself more comic than real. If the UGC had any ability it could have woken up to the challenge of foreign invasion on the Indian academic ground. While the UGC and the Ministry of HRD are lost in their astrological warfare, foreign universities and institutions of doubtful credibility are merrily going about doing their business as usual, unchallenged for the past one decade as if there is no government in the country. One could go on adding to the list of failures of this moribund system called the UGC and the manner in which it has lost credibility in the eyes of those who have still some capacity to think. Surely, the UGC could be complimented for providing comic relief to those who otherwise remain ever so morose and serious only to appear academic. Some one needs to do some serious research to find a single achievement to the credit of the UGC. If one did find something of the sort he is sure to be noticed by the powers that be.

The need of the hour is to think whether or not any change is possible in the system and if it is possible how soon will that change take place. I therefore have a dream. I would like this dream to become a reality. This paper was presented before representatives from the Ministry of HRD, UGC and the Planning Commission, besides experts who reminded us that there are other matters too that need immediate consideration. For instance, the challenges like the Intellectual Property Rights, the IT and ICT, the presence of foreign universities in India, paucity of funds, privatization of education versus public funding etc. Therefore, there are several problems that face the nation but being what we are I am quite sure none will be resolved. The solutions may be expected only when problems are well passed resolution stage.

Meanwhile, I suggest a few points for improvement.

My recommendations are as follows:

a) All colleges in the country may be allowed to become autonomous in the sense that they may teach the courses evolved by them. They may conduct their own examinations and evaluate and issue certificates. The esteem of each college will be made to depend on the patronage these institutions will come to earn in due course of time.

b) The economically non-viable colleges will have the freedom to evolve suitable measures to become viable. In this process of becoming viable all options for raising funds may be left open to them.

c) The selection of the teachers will be the responsibility of the each governing body. These committees will normally follow the guidelines provided either by the NAAC or their own federation at the state or the center.

d) The maintenance of these colleges will entirely be the responsibility of each governing body. The State or the Center may patronize any or a few of these colleges for their excellence or singular achievement.

e) A system be evolved to reward each year a minimum number of institutions with monetary help both for recognition as well as growth.

f) As each college will have to be assessed through either by NAAC or some other system developed for the purpose almost on a five year basis the inter or intra transfers of students during transfers of guardians or change of residence for some other cause will not be seriously affected.

g) These colleges will be encouraged to become innovative in imparting academic skills and acquisition of knowledge. For instance, the starting of each course will not always pre-suppose the appointment of a regular faculty. The techniques already in practice in BITS, Pilani could serve as a model.

h) The high-tech teaching assistance mode should be adopted for cutting down the cost of modernization of courses and for effective instruction. The initial cost of installing expensive equipment in these colleges be subsidized in the deserving cases under a reasonable frame of arrangement.

i) All colleges be encouraged to have on their governing bodies representatives of various industries and interests. This will help these institutions become responsive to social and business requirements.

j) The principals of these colleges will meet at the regional, state and the center level according to an arrangement mutually agreed upon for coordination and development. .

k) It may be worthwhile to consider that all these institutions whether in the region or the state should be made to so distribute their areas of specialization that in future they may become centers of excellence.

l) Teachers of one college should have the option with the consent of the governing body to share their knowledge or skill from time to time with the students of other colleges.

m) Teachers should be free on payment to the institution concerned to start their individual courses provided such teaching or the offering does not duplicate or interfere with the college's efforts. This will effectively control and reduce the clientele of the teaching shops.

If the Government accepts this scheme, which is very doubtful, as proposed the universities will be freed from this additional charge and thus undertake meaningful research which not unlike the ones being undertaken in the agricultural universities will have social, material and policy impact. Also then the UGC for its own survival (it will survive because where else will the government have their favorites find places with no work?) will have to develop a more responsive and academic role.

The real idea is that all colleges may be allowed freedom from the stranglehold of the UGC. In fact the colleges be organized at the state level. The State may not give any grant to them. All that it needs to have is an agency of voluntary efforts to reward institutions of merit in every way possible. The non-viable institutions may be allowed to die out. The Darwinian principle of the survival of the fittest be allowed to operate.

The real danger for the bad, non-viable institutions come from e-learning and online courses. The download.com is a greater threat to these colleges and several universities than the inefficient teaching and the incompetence of their staffs.

Somehow, it is necessary to remember that each age has a challenge of its own and each challenge its own matching solution. There is hardly any need to get panicky. This nation too will survive its present managers and planners. While the vast majority of them will have fallen by the wayside and get overlooked by History, the nation will go on living. These wise men will have the satisfaction that they too lived when their nation faced a challenge; their misery will only be that they never acted when it was possible to do so.

I am grateful to all my friends and well wishers who helped me to bring this volume out. Its acceptance will depend on those who are thinking beings. For the rest, my best wishes.

Professor R.P.Singh
A-4/206, Kalkaji Extension,
New Delhi-110019

INTRODUCTION

Dr. G D Sharma

In an International Conference on Higher Education organised by Education International in collaboration with UNESCO, Paris, it was stated that "governments want more people to go in higher education,but they also want to keep public spending down",consequently"curriculum development has been turned over to commercial interest."Higher Education *per se* is faced with this dual problem. Besides, India is the only country which has a system of "affiliating colleges". We continue with this colonial heritage because the way out suggested by Dr. S. Radhakrishnan in his report as early as 1948 and by the Indian Education Commission in 1964-66 followed by NPE 1986 did not attract many which Malcolm Adisheshiah had wanted it to. He was very clear in his mind that without Autonomous Colleges, Higher Education in India would collapse under it own weight. One would suspect the real causes of slowness in colleges becoming autonomous lie in certain apprehensions, doubts and on uncertainties besides the fear of having sudden freedom.

A Seminar was recently organised precisely for this reason of alleying fears and building confidence in the concept.The University Grants Commission has held seminars on autonomous colleges earlier on as well.This time there were two reasons: a) we are moving into an information age therefore the pace of innovations has to be both comprehensive and fast, and b) autonomous degree granting colleges alone can look after the local / regional interests. A university is too big a system to attend to the interests, problems and challenges that its colleges may face. Consequent obligation naturally rests on the colleges themselves who must learn to look after themselves. This conference was however distinct from the earlier ones as principals and representatives of almost all the autonomous colleges attended the conference and shared their experiences.

Secretary, UGC

The future of higher education lies with autonomous colleges which ultimately must offer need-based courses without seeking anybody's approval except their own. The possibilities and potentialities as one looks at the prospects of these colleges are simply too enormous to count.

The paper presented by the Chairperson, UGC, details both the anxieties and potentialities that these colleges carry within themselves. Participation of delegates was very effective and forward looking. The recommendations made by them come out of very intense debate, discussion and experiences of this concept.

One could only hope the colleges which are as yet outside the fold of 'autonomy' will come forward and embrace it in full measure and permit the nation to have the advantage of their intellect as well as innovations.

We must face the problem of viability of and the quality of education being offered by them. Perhaps the answer to this question lies in the Accreditation criteria and the regular grading of all institutions at the national level. All this is not only going to provide quality education, but also a kind of vibrancy and the desire to compete which may help India meet the challenges faced by it in the present and future contexts.

The future holds promise and has the potential, then why do we not meet the challenges boldly and squarely? Let us not turn back from the dawn of tomorrow lest our posterity accuse us for our lack of vision and courage.

CHAPTER 1

WHITHER AUTONOMY: ITS PLACE - TODAY AND TOMORROW

Dr. (Miss) A. S. Desai*

It is with a great deal of anticipation that I have looked forward to this conference and welcome everyone to participate in this unique and exciting experiment to support autonomy in the educational system. The UGC looks forward to your contribution in the discussions and the recommendations. We are very grateful to Dr. J.V. Narlikar, Director, Inter-University Centre for Astronomy and Astro-Physics, for collaborating with us in this effort, by making their infrastructure and personnel available. The responsibility for its local organisation has been taken by Dr. N.K.Jain, Joint Secretary, Western Regional Office, in collaboration with the University of Pune and IUCAA. They have made all arrangements for us to meet in these very conductive surroundings. Dr. K. Gunasekaran, Joint Secretary, Southern Regional Office, took the responsibility for the academic and programmatic aspects of the Conference. We appreciate the efforts of all these Houses in organising the Conference.

The Concept of Autonomy

The concept of autonomy is not new. It has been with us since 1948 (University Education Commission headed by the president of India, Dr. S. Radhakrishnan, himself a teacher), the committee on Colleges, headed by Prof. Mahajani, the Committee on Standards of University Education, headed by Prof. S.K. Sidhartha, 1965, the Gajendragadkar Committee on Governance of Universities and Colleges and the Kothari Commission of 1966. It was further reiterated in our National Policy on Education in 1986.

---

* Chairperson, University Grants Commission, Bahadur Shah Zafar Marg, New Delhi-2. Welcome address and Opening remarks at the Conference on "Autonomous Colleges in the 21st Century", held by the UGC at the Inter-University Centre for Astronomy and Astro-Physics on the campus of Pune University, November 9 to 11, 1998.

In spite of 50 years (from 1948 to 1998) of reiteration of the theme of autonomy, it has not taken root while our erstwhile rulers, the British, who imposed on us the system then prevailing in London University, have long abandoned it. The "permit" raj still continues to rule our educational system by enforcing the affiliating system which, besides imposing a rigid structure, at times an outdated syllabus, and an examination based on memorization, is able to do little else, as such, for the colleges. It is a system which has spawned guide books and teaching shops because the major focus is competitive examinations, based on memorization, inducing subject rather than student centred learning. Yet, thousands of teachers and managements in this country, not to speak of university administrations and state governments, continue to cling to the system which has been fraught with so many problems, both academic and administrative.

Academic autonomy leads to the empowerment of teachers. The objective is to give the necessary freedom for a group of teachers to decide the vision and the mission of the organization, set objectives, design the inputs through a relevant curriculum, decide the appropriate method of imparting it, and devise the best method of evaluating the outcome, so that, knowlegde, skills and attitudes, the key objectives of education, can be tested more effectively. This is the major reason to encourage autonomy for the college, while all the connected bodies, that is, the management of the college, the parent university, the State Government, and the UGC, must support this effort through their respective roles. Thus, the role of the college management is to provide freedom and flexibility in a framework of democratic decision making, to empower the teachers to achieve the objective of academic autonomy, for which, both the teachers and the management are equally accountable. A conducive environment is necessary to practice autonomy, in the spirit in which it has been conceived, in order to increase both the relevance and the quality of education.

Some Fears Related to Autonomy

There are some notions which have impeded the development of autonomy. The question asked is why, if it is so good, it has not been replicated in many institutions. It is assumed that something is wrong with the model rather than asking whether our own process of socialization makes it difficult for us to accept it such as the teacher's need for seeking security in a rigid structure and the management's inability to induce democratic and responsible behaviours in management- teacher relationships. After 50 years, on the eve of the

IXth Plan,there were only 119 colleges (March, 1997) and, a year later, we have 123 with a few more in the pipe-line. The possible impeding factors are:

1. In the early decades, teachers faced insecurity which has made them cling to the affiliating system, possibly in the belief that the university, and the teacher's associations, would give them protection against any arbitrary hiring and firing practices. However, with the type of university rules prevailing today, in fact, such fears are unfounded as they equally apply to an autonomous college. Moreover, autonomy is not for equiping managements for arbitrary action in personnel practice. It also does not at all prevent teachers from being members of a teacher's organization if they should seek security in numbers.

2. Another objection is that it leads to additional work. However, let us ask ourselves whether our salaries are for minimum performance or maximum? It is a fact that the public image of teachers in the higher education system is negative. The public believes that teachers work only half the year for half the working day for a full salary. Over the decades, we have struggled to obtain a better deal for our teachers with respect to salaries and other conditions of service, but we also have to fulfil our obligations to the community which pays these costs and, most of all, trusts us with the future of our citizens.

3. There is a belief that only elitist institutions will benefit from autonomy and, therefore, it will suffer from inequity. The response to this issue has been to depress everyone to the lowest common denominator which is not the way to promote equity. I am sure that it is no one's brief that poorer quality education has to be nurtured to promote equity. In fact, it would improve education by conferring autonomy on those who can function well with it, so that, the university is freed to pay attention to those whose performance needs greater inputs and encouragement for improving quality. The scheme does not rule out colleges which attract students from disadvantaged groups or rural communities. Their performance may not be high because of the poor school system from which they graduate. But, the college must show how it is making efforts through currricular reforms, teaching methods, and co-curricular activities, which remedy the past disadvantages and empower its students for the future. It is the demonstration of the accademic innovations taken by its teachers, their genuine desire to improve their programme, and the concern of its management to back it up, which is of the most importance. In fact, autonomy to such colleges can further equip them to tailor the programme to the needs of their

students, so that, it is relevant. Greater qualitative inputs can be made with appropriate opportunities for the teachers to upgrade their own capacities.

A University, which is freed from a larger section of its colleges, can provide the necessary attention to those which need its assistance not being bogged down by the examination of a large number of students, it can give the necessary time for inspection of the colleges, instead of examination of the students, and through the College Development Council, if appropriately strengthened, provide the necessary inputs to its colleges particularly needing attention. Affiliation, then, can be a more positive instrument for development of those requiring such attention. In fact, it is wrongly assumed that all such weak institutions will be closed down. Would there be any reason to close an institution which shows by its actions that it means business? Those weeded out are the unviable ones whose meagre student and staff strength, and a lack of desire to contribute to making a college an institution of higher education does not, in any case, justify their existence. Goodwill of society will be earned, not by keeping colleges prisoners of a system which has many problems, but where a large number of institutions are freed to perform their best, while those needing attention are given necessary assistance by their university.

There are some other accusations. One such accusation is the reliability of examination marking, but this is equally in doubt in the affiliating system anyway. Another is the pressure of institutional authorities, students and parents, when, in fact, in the present affiliating system, the serious students and parents have abdicated their responsbility to demand a relevant and qualitative education. Another accusation is the harassment of students by teachers which would occur as a result of internal marks system. However, it is noted that almost all institutions have both internal and external systems of evaluation and, hence, any internal marks of a student, either high or low over the external, would show up the discrepancy.

I would like this conference to discuss these issues and bring out the positive and the truly negative aspects, if any, of an autonomous system, so that, not only such doubts are clarified but also the negatives can be corrected so that the system of autonomy can fully expand to encompass a large number of institutions. Principals were also once teachers and, drawn from that community. They should see autonomy from the perspective of the teacher and how best any correctives can be applied, so that, a larger number of institutions can enjoy the fruits of autonomy.

The Positive Aspects of Autonomy

As a preparation for this conference, the colleges were asked to respond to a proforma which elicited information on the unique features adopted by the college enjoying autonomy. Curious to know what they felt they had achieved, I went through the responses which had been received and sent to me, from the two southern States of Tamil Nadu and Andhra Pradesh. These responses made interesting reading. It was most heartening to see that they had made changes in the curriculum to meet local area needs; and many opportunities were made available for co-curricular activities leading to both skills and the personality development of the students. The colleges and their teachers are to be congratulated on their tremendous inputs to make education both relevant and qualitative. Contrary to fears expressed in some quarters that the quality of education would go down,in fact, the quality of education has shown a marked improvement as borne out by the reviews conducted in the institutions, once in five years, by the UGC.

It is not how students compete and score which is important in education, though that has become the sole criterion, but how far education responds to students' needs and how far it leads to their development as persons who are to enter the adult world as citizens, as family makers, and as bread winners. If the autonomous colleges achieve in the development of a well rounded human being, capable of being an informed citizen, with a developed social consciousness for living in a pluralistic social order, a democratic and non-exploitative social structure which emphasises protection of human rights and environment, we would have achieved the right priorities for education. Thus, the belief that students should have an opportunity to sit for a university examination, so that they can compete with others and achieve laurels,which, in any case, only a few at the top can get, most of whom will be from advantageous backgrounds, is a non-requirement for quality education.

The responses reveal that innovation and change have been the major achievements of autonony. In the first instance, the courses have undergone considerable modification. The institutions offer core courses, optionals, as also courses beyond the required number, for which the student can earn extra credits. A number of application oriented subjects are emerging, some of them interdisciplinary.

The subjects include:

- Computer orientation in almost all the courses;
- Wild-Life Biology, Biochemistry, Environmental Botany, Medical Botany, Plant Products;
- Environmental Chemistry, Petroleum and Petro Products, Mineral Exploration (in Geology) and Household Chemistry.
- Mineral Bonification and Materials Handling, Drilling Technology, Synthetic Drugs, Adulterants in Foods.
- B.E. Mechatronics (four year course)
- Aqua-culture in Zoology
- In Economics or Commerce: Advertising, Sales and Sales Promotion, Publicity, Taxation Practice, Consumer Education, Office Management and Secretarial Practice, Entrepreneurship
- Industrial Psychology
- Health Care and Hospital Management
- Tourism in history courses.

Some unusual courses include:

- Science of Creativity and Personality Development
- Mathematics for Non-Mathematics Students
- Regional/Local events/personalities contributing to the freedom struggle
- Life oriented education for the empowerment of women
- Women's writing.

Some of the rural based colleges, or those close to rural locations, have developed various programmes. Such colleges are fewer but, we hope that, in time, more autonomous colleges will be established in rural areas. One of them is working on documenting kolums, folk songs, lullaby songs and proverbs to preserve the local culture. Another has a full degree course in farm science and rural development with field practicals. **Almost all autonomous colleges report changes in syllabus within periods of 2 to 4 years.**

Many of the colleges give additional certificate and diploma courses to enrich their students which range from photography to yoga and ISTD. They have foundation courses to include understanding of the local area, women's studies and environment studies, science for students in humanities and social sciences, and humanities and social science for those in the sciences.

The structure has been changed to semester and credit system in several colleges and introduction of viva voce and project work as part of the evaluation. Most of them have both internal and external examinations and some have elaborate methods of handling differences in marks between the internal and external. All use continuous and semester end examinations. Testing and evaluation are linked to assignments, seminars, quiz, crosswords, open book tests, objective type as also short and long answers in the examinations, and development of a question bank. Several have required project work. Many use the system of centralised evaluation and prompt publication of results. Some allow students to reappear to improve results and a few allow students to see their answer scripts should they question their results.

The teaching methods are equally varied with the use of audio-visuals, multi-media, project work, demonstration, group discussion, debates, students' presentation and peer group learning, games and role play, self-study, seminars, and industrial attachment. almost all have bought the necessary audio-visual equipment from the UGC grant.

A few have some special features like a Grievance Cell for students, the tutor-ward system for guidance, Guidance and Counselling Centre, campus interviews and placements (job) and internet. Several have automated their examinations and also office procedures. Attendance is compulsory and in some cases, students weak in studies are given extra coaching. One institution has a creche facility. Many have faculty committees, one has a study circle, and one college trains new teachers in effective communication.

Extension activities are reported by a number of institutions such as Science and Humanities for People's Development, Student Training and Action for Neighbourhood Development, Taking Science to Rural Areas, community extension services, Adult and Population Education, Women's Cell, NCC and NSS.

It is very satisfying to note that the colleges are striving to give the best to their students and the increased workload is not an impediment. In fact, some report the satisfaction teachers feel in their achievement, in a good job well done.

Future Thrust

I believe that several thousand colleges have the potential to do well and establish the credibility of the higher education system. In the twenty-first century, they will need to develop the student for not only a vocation or a career but to function in a knowledge based society for which they will have to learn how to access knowledge and utilise it not only for their own benefit but for the society at large. They need to place more emphasis on the college as a community institution for life-long learning attracting students of all ages and of all socio-economic groups. Autonomy connotes flexibility. They can offer a wide variety of programmes to target groups from young to old, from those who can enter our formal system to those who can access our many other programmes offered by the college to respond to specific community needs for those who would, otherwise, not be the candidates of our formal system.

We need to develop vigorous extension programmes by which our knowledge and skills will be used in the service of others. We need to activate every department to reach out and focus on issues which affect the local community. College must become a community institution, a focal point for interaction and development of the community addressing itself to community concerns and needs.

In the end, our students of the twenty-first century must usher in an era of non-violence which means a non-exploitative social structure of equity and social justice in which unity is created even in diversity as tolerance and respect for differences, human worth and dignity, create a community of persons who aspire to build a society of dynamic stability where every person has the opportunity to use his/her capacity to the fullest.

Chapter 2
On Autonomy For Colleges

Prof G.J.V Jagannadharaju, Chancellor, Sri Chandra Shekharendra Saraswati Vishvavidyalaya, Kanchipuram - 631552

Developement of human resources through education and training is undoubtedly the need of the hour in a populous country like India. Human Resource Development serves not only as an instrument of social change but also as an effective and powerful tool to usher in a major transformation enabling us to look upon the teeming millions not as a burden but as national wealth. A mammoth task of this magnitude calls for huge expansion in education system at all levels. Indeed, there has been phenomenal expansion during the last few decades, but compared with the requirements of the next century the task ahead is stupendous. In 1947, when India got independence, there were only 19 universities and 636 colleges with a student enrolment of about one lakh six thousand. Since then, there has been tremendous upsurge in the demand for higher education resulting in a significant growth in the number of universities and colleges. Today there are over 230 universities and university-level institutions and about 10,500 colleges. The annual growth rate is about 5 percent. The student population is around five million, and there are over three lakh teachers. We have institutions with different type of management structures. There are Central Universities, Institutions of National Importance, State Universities, Institutions deemed to be Universities, Regional Colleges, Government Colleges, Aided Colleges, Unaided Colleges and Self-financing Colleges. Some of the institutions are comparable with the best in the rest of the world. With 85% of the students population being in the affiliated colleges, there has been an abnormal increase in the number of affiliated colleges in each University making the system unwieldy and unmanageable. The unprecedented expansion, particularly during the last two decades, has resulted in the mushrooming of institutions in higher education, breeding mediocrity. Higher education in India is to-day beset with the problems such as:

Quantitative expansion at the expense of quality mismatch between the output and the manpower needs of job market -- unemployment and unemployability of graduates -- wide disparities in the quality of institutions -- lack of relevance and flexibility in curriculum -- lack of choice of courses in the requirements for a degree -- lack of continuous assessment for evaluation -- many institutions resist change and are reluctant to break the shackles of the traditional approach.

The affiliating system does not permit the freedom or flexibility required by the colleges to introduce changes in the curriculum fast enough to respond to the needs of the society. It does not allow the colleges to introduce innovations in developing new courses and changes in the system of evaluation which is vitally important in moulding the study habits of the students.

As a remedial measure, granting autonomy to selected institutions had been under discussion for a long time. Autonomy implies not only freedom but also accountability . Autonomy aims at empowering the colleges to develop new courses which are employment oriented and are relevant to social needs, to introduce innovations in curriculum development in the various courses of study, to make meaningful innovations in the teaching- learning process through the active involvement of teachers and students, to introduce examination reforms, to promote employment skills and to bring in such other changes required for improving the quality of education.

Autonomy brings in decentralisation and quick response to societal needs and permits the colleges to take up the challenges to strive hard for achieving excellence.

Recognising the need for granting autonomy to an outstanding college or a cluster of very good colleges, the Education Commission (Kothari Commission -- 1964-66) recommended that provision be made for creation of autonomous colleges in the constitution of Universities to empower such colleges to frame their own rules of admission (consistent with the rules of reservation), to prescribe the courses of study, to conduct examination etc.

Accepting the concept of granting autonomy, to select colleges, the University Grants Commission initiated steps but the response was not encouraging.

Tamilnadu took an early lead in the sphere of Autonomous Colleges and it continues to maintain its lead till date. In the year 1978-79, University of Madras granted autonomous status to eight of its affiliated colleges and Madurai Kamraj University to two of its colleges.

In pursuance of the emphasis laid on the implementation of the scheme of Autonomous Colleges by the National Policy on Education, the University Grants Commission issued detailed revised guidelines 1986) in this regard.

Consequently a few Universities in some of the States initiated steps to grant autonomy to a few selected colleges under their jurisdiction. However, only few colleges came forward and even this was confined to a couple of States in the Southern Region. In recent years, the momentum has started picking up, though it is not at all upto the expectations.

To-date, there are 124 Autonomous Colleges in the Country, spread over eight States only, under the jurisdiction of 28 Universities. Out of these, 107 colleges are in three of the States - Tamilnadu, Madhya Pradesh and Andhra Pradesh and they account for 86% of the Autonomous Colleges. There are 48 Autonomous Colleges in Tamilnadu alone which form about 39% of the total number, 40 in Madhya Pradesh which constitutes 32, and 19 in Andhra Pradesh which constitutes 15%. The position in other States is as follows:

Orissa and Himachal Pradesh	-	5 each
Maharashtra and U.P	-	3 each
Gujarat	-	1

These statistics reveal that the concept of Autonomy and its merits have not percolated in most of the States. Several apprehensions/ misconceptions in the minds of the educational administrators, the teachers and the supporting staff are perhaps major causes for the prevalence of such a situation. At the same time it is noteworthy that, in recent times, there is a demand for conferment of autonomous status from more and more colleges in the States in which a good number of autonomous colleges already exist. It is essential that the causes for these trends be analysed carefully, so that steps could be taken to effectively spread the concept of Autonomous Colleges in the States in which little or absolutely no progress has been made.

If we note that only 1.5% of the colleges in the country are implementing the scheme of autonomous colleges, the huge magnitude of the task to be undertaken by the UGC together with the states and the universities concerned in improving the situation becomes evident. Resistance to change due to inertia, fears or misconceptions appear to be the main contributing factors and to overcome the same, a clear idea of the different types of apprehensions misconceptions lurking in the minds of people concerned is necessary. The major ones among them are:

1. In the conventional system, the University concerned is vested with the power to make or alter the academic regulations as a central authority whereas this power is decentralised in the scheme of Autonomous Colleges. The authorities which make these regulations are within easy reach of the students who might have a tendency to launch agitations for dilution of regulations and for the postponement of examinations. The managements and the teaching community feel, that it is a tremendous responsibility and it may be very difficult for them to withstand these pressures.

2. The system leaves room for nepotism, favouritism and victimisation of students because of the features inherent in the evaluation system wherever Continuous Internal Assessment System is introduced.

3. It creates two different classes of institutions, the autonomous colleges being the elitist among them.

4. It imposes a heavy financial responsibility on the management which have to bear the burden of creating additional physical facilities and additional manpower.

5. Due to the introduction of internal assessment and tutorials there will be considerable increase in the workload and the responsibilities of the teachers. The teachers will have to shed their inertia in tuning themselves to effective and improved methods of teaching.

6. Due to lack of uniformity in the content of curriculum and the system of evaluation and due to the consequent absence of a basis for comparison of the products of different colleges under the jurisdiction of the same university, the acceptability of the students for higher studies, inter-collegiate transfers and for employment becomes questionable.

The actual experiences narrated and the facts that have emerged from the deliberations at various workshops, visits and review exercises carried out (by NIEPA -1986-87; Tamilnadu Government - 1990: APSCHE - 1990-91: SRO- 1995-96), in respect of the colleges which are already implementing the scheme, however, reveal that such fears and misgivings can be allayed by the adoption of procedures which ensure transparency, by the provision of build - in checks and balances and by devising suitable remedial measures wherever necessary. I am sure that such exercises should have been conducted in Madhya Pradesh and other places.

Regading fears about student pressures for dilution of regulations, it is observed, on the contrary, that the student attendance, discipline and interaction with teachers have improved to a great extent and there is appreciation of the benefit of continous internal assessment system particularly in terms of better knowledge inputs and greater effectiveness in teaching-learning process in the autonomous colleges.

In continuous assessment, credibility can be established only when the assessment gains acceptance from the students on the basis of total transparency. The actual experence shows that well-designed procedures can lead to a foolproof system in which possibilities of favouritism or victimisation are eliminated.

Elitism among educational institutions, if achieved through attainment of excellence, deserves to be promoted and there is absolutely no need to be apologetic about it. Thus, there is no merit in the argument that the scheme of Autonomous Colleges creates an elitist class of institutions. Even without the creation of Autonomous Colleges, there are bound to be different classes of colleges based on the reputation gained by them through excellence. They cannot be wished away.

Having recognised the fact that the Autonomous Colleges deserve financial assistance to the extent of the additional burden imposed on them due to the requirement of additional physical facilities and manpower, University Grants Commission has been extending support as per norms laid down for this purpose. University Grants Commission may consider apportioning some amount out of the provisions for its schemes/ programmes such as Special Assistance, Travel Grant, Faculty Improvement etc. for autonomous colleges.

The conduct of common entrance test by each University for admission to Post Graduate Courses renders it superfluous to compare the qualifying examination marks, be it external or internal. Thus, variations in evaluation system adopted by different Autonomous colleges do not pose any problem.

I am happy to note that one full session is being devoted to innovation and change under autonomy at this conference. I hope that the deliberations will focus attention on:

(i) modification of the curriculum with emphasis on relevance,

(ii) assignment of field oriented projects pertaining to live problems,

(iii) quantum of internal assessment for evaluation together with procedures to be adopted for ensuring transparency,

(iv) formats for obtaining student feedback for improving the quality of teaching process.

The session on TQM- HRD, I am sure will highlight the importance of various aspects of accreditation as applied in particular to autonomous colleges.

At the session which is devoted to problems of administration, finance and relationship between Colleges - Universities - Government and UGC, problems such as

(i) additional workload and requirement of additional manpower,

(ii) methods of ensuring prompt filling up of vacant teaching posts,

(iii) requirement of additional financial inputs,

(iv) establishment of Academic Staff Colleges exclusively for autonomous colleges for organising orientation and refresher courses and training programmes at regular intervals,

(v) constitution of co-ordinating bodies such as Autonomous Colleges Council at State/University level for liaison between the Colleges, University, Government and UGC,and

(vi) constitution of appeals and grievance committee as a statutory body, deserve to be discussed threadbare.

I am of the opinion that every one of these institutions should prepare perspective plans both long range and short range and through annual self-appraisals the level of realisation may be noted. Sharing of experiences and resources among a group of colleges will be useful.

Abolition of the affiliation system is inevitable some day or the other and the sooner this is realised the better. No one expects this major task to be achieved overnight. The major challenge to be faced in the 21st century in the sphere of higher education, as I envisage, is total abolition of the affiliating system and evolving an alternative for replacing it. The concept of autonomous colleges has to be taken to its logical conclusion by giving the power of conferring their own degrees to such of these colleges which are able to establish their credibility. In the case of smaller degree colleges which do not have a broad spectrum of faculties a cluster of limited number of colleges may perhaps be kept under the jurisdiction of an Academic Board with powers to confer the degrees under the seal of the Board. Each institution will have to establish its own credibility and earn its own reputation by striving for excellence. If the goal of an institution is to achieve excellence in teaching, research, consultancy, extension, administration, linkages and placements, one has to adopt total quality management principles. The institutions are to work towards improving their quality, increasing their effectiveness and continuously strive towards excellence. Accreditation will have to play an important role by ranking or classifying these institutions based on their performance. The massive programme for creation of awareness of the benefits of scheme of Autonomous Colleges will have to be launched particularly in the states where no progress has been made till date. Such a programme should aim at convincing all concerned to introduce or strengthen, as the case may be, the autonomous colleges by the turn of the century. Review at frequent intervals is essential and modification to guidelines where ever and whenever necessary should be incorporated based on the feedback from these reviews.

I wish to conclude with the observation, that the autonomous colleges have made a significant mark in bringing out some innovations in curriculum development, introduction of restructured and job-oriented courses and even in conventional courses the syllabi is updated and made more relevant through introduction of new topics. These institutions, except in a very few cases, introduced examination reforms and the teaching-learning process is made more effective. This being the situation, I am of the strong opinion that, unless we get rid of the present archaic system of affiliation, we have no hope of facing the demands of the next century in the worldwide educational scene.

CHAPTER 3
SHRI DATTAJI RANE

The Minister For Higher and Technical Education, Maharashtra

Chairperson, University Grants Commission, Prof, A.S.Desai, Shri P.R.Dasgupta, Secretary, Government of India, Ministry of Human Resource Development, Prof. Nigwekar, Prof. Naralikar, Prof. Raju, Dr. Jain, other dignitaries and participants. The Western Regional Office of U.G.C. at Pune deserves to be congratulated on convening this Conference on" Autonomy of Colleges in 21st Century" and giving us all an opportunity for exchanging our views with every one present here.

Along with you, I am also concerned about the long-term perspectives of the concept of Autonomy for the colleges. Autonomy is the power or right to self-Government. Autonomy is also the 'free-will' that carries within itself the guiding principles for action. This 'free-will' has to be developed in every human being and education is the means for the development of this 'free-will'. It is deliverance from dependence that is the aim of true education.

We are all now set in quest for quality in higher education. The present debate and dilemma about quality in higher education can possibly be best understood within the dynamic complex relationships between the society, state and higher education system. Autonomy to educational institutions has all along been considered as a vehicle to cruise through smoothly towards quality and excellence.

When you are in the process of discussing what kind of Autonomy to Colleges in the 21st Century, I would like to place some points before you for consideration. These may be some stray thoughts but they also could be important.

The Autonomous Colleges are relieved from the University structure with a freedom to determine their own courses of study. In the process, the Autonomous Colleges have to develop the principles of governance of the institution independently. The teacher being the agent of change and dynamism has a great role to play in the success of Autonomous Colleges. The teacher has to be equipped himself with necessary tools in promoting the academic excellence among the students keeping in mind the societal needs. Academic excellence among the students is basically to discourage cramming, helping him to develop curiosity and creativity relevant to the society, to himself. The teacher also needs training to deliver this additional workload and responsibility.

Governance in Autonomous Colleges calls for drastic changes in attitudes and functions. The question arises whether Autonomous Colleges have the organisational competence and financial support to fulfill this objective. Participatory role of all the members concerned and doing away with the authoritative style can alone complete the democratisation of educational atmosphere.

When we are at the doorsteps of the next millennium, it is also the time to retrospect, reflect and renew. The experienced colleges with years of autonomy must reflect upon how they have managed the autonomy so far. This will help in realising prevalence of an effective and responsible autonomy.

Autonomous Colleges are said to be pioneering, innovative, pace setting and ensuring quality improvement. We must assess as to what exactly we have pioneered? How have we ensured quality improvement? To what extent the experienced autonomous colleges have set the pace for upcoming autonomous colleges ?

I thank you all for giving me this opportunity to express my views and anxiety.

Chapter 4

Redesigning of Curriculum

Dr. SR. Annamma Philip, FMM

Over the last few decades there have been remarkable changes in the educational system in India and many of these changes have been related to the curriculum. The credit based system has been in vogue in the USA for the last 4 decades and has been adopted by many Institutes like the IIT's REC's and a few Autonomous Colleges. The traditional system in India follows marking system with equal weightage. In some cases marks are converted to grades and Grade Point Average to OGPA. The credit system is one in which differential weightage is given to courses in terms of hours of study but is directly correlated to the courses content. Here the students' performance in an examination gets assigned with the credit points of that course. The evaluation can be reported either in terms of marks or grades or both.

In this system the student centred approach to learning is emphasized and they are given opportunities to pursue an integrated programme at their own pace in keeping with their ability and aptitude.

The main objective of the system is to:

____ to provide broad based education

____ to provide students with greater flexibility in choice of courses

____ to enable students to choose courses at basic/advanced levels

____ to enable students to progress at their own pace

____ to enable highly motivated students gain extra credits

'Credit': The term credit describes the quantum of syllabi for various programmes in terms of hours of study. It indicated differential weightage given according to the content and duration of the course in the curriculum design.

Principal, Stella Marris College, Chennai

And given degree programme should have a minimum number of credit requirement, for e.g. A Bachelor's degree could have approxiamately 90 credits. Institutions should afford students opportunity to earn extra credits.

'Courses': Each course designed may comprise lectures/ tutorials/ laboratory work/ seminar/ project work/ on-the job training, etc. to meet effective teaching and learning needs and credits are assigned suitably.

A degree programme consists of a number of courses : a set of compulsory courses (*core* courses) and a set of *Optional/elective* courses.

Core courses are basic requirements for each discipline. *Elective/Optional* courses may be offered by a department for its own students or to students of other departments.

Course weightage: In the credit based system, each course offered is assigned a weightage of certain number of credits e.g., there could be courses of 1, 2, 3, or 4 credits. The number of credits assigned pertains to the course content and is related to duration of each course. Core and elective courses may carry different weightages. For example a course carrying 2 credits for lectures, will have instruction of two hours per week, during the semester. If a course requires 3 hours of lecture per week then it will be considered as a 3 credit course. Credits are assigned on the basis of the number of lecture/ laboratory work and other forms of learning in a semester.

The weithtage of credits may vary for lecture/laboratory work/ seminar/project, etc. For e.g. One credit for each lecture hour per week.

One credit for each tutorial hour per week (in certain cases Tutorial need not be given weightage)

One credit for every 2/3 hours of Laboratory/practical work per week

One credit for every 3 contact hours for project work' in a week

One credit for every 2 hours of seminar conducted

4/5 credits for dissertation! project work in the final semester (inclusive of viva voce).

Code and Course Components

Code: Courses are coded in a manner where in the department offering the course, type of course (Core 7 Optional), the title of the course, the semester when offered and the : number of credits is incorporated. For example

HS/ MC / AH 13

HS : Department of History MC : Major Core

AH : Ancient History (Title of Paper)

13 : The first digit '1' Semester when the course is offered the second digit '3' indicates the number of credits assigned to the course.

Components: The number of credits assigned per course is equal to the number of lecture hours per week. Each course may entail a certain number of tutorial hours per week, for example a 3 credit course involves 3 lecture hours and 1 or 2 tutorial hours per week. The courses also denote components of L, T, P, C where L=Lecture. T=Tutorial and P=Practical/Project work, C=Total Credit.

For example:	L T P C	L T P C	L T P C
	3003	0021	4104

For theory papers L=C and for practical papers-2 hours of Practical work=C

CREDIT PATTERN ADOPTED IN STELLA MARIS COLLEGE, CHENNAI.

ALLOTMENT OF CREDITS FOR AN UNDERGRADUATE PROGRAMME

		CREDITS		
		Offered	A Student can earn Max.	Min.
Part I				
Language	- Core	9	9	9
	- Optional	5	3	–
Part II				
English	- Core	5	5	5
	- Optional	8	4	4
Part III				
Major	- Core	40	40	40
	- Optional	12	12	6
Allied	- Core	12	12	12
	- Optional	6	6	3
Part IV				
a) General Electives		110	12	6
b) Value Education		5	3	3
c) Social Awareness Programme		12	4	2
Part V				
a) Student Training Programmes (NSS/NCC/Games)		26	6	2
b) Professional & Skill Development Programmes		8	4	—
TOTAL			**120**	**92**

To qualify for the degree in 3 years a student is required to earn an average of 15 credits per semester. Students are expected to register and complete: the course requirement for a minimum of 12 credits per semester.

Registration of Courses: Students are required to register for the course.

The Faculty Advisers counsel the students on matters regarding choice of courses, withdrawal, etc. The students must meet the Faculty Adviser at least 2 times in a semester.

Departmental Committee

Every Department should have a departmental committee consisting of:

1. The Faculty members of the department
2. 3/4 student representatives from each class
3. The Academic Dean- (s)
4. The Dean (s) for Curriculum Development
5. The Vice-Principal (s) The Controller of Examinations and Faculty teaching Foundation Courses (Language and English) may be invited.

The department committee should meet at least twice in a semester to review the academic programme.

Classification of Successful Candidates

Classification will be based on Credit Weighted Average

$$\text{Credit Weight Average (CWA)} = \frac{\text{\% of Marks x Credits}}{\text{Total Credits earned by students}}$$

The class obtained by students are indicated on a Cumulative Mark Statement issued to them on successful completion of the degree programme.

A List of General Electives Offered in Stella Marris College.

Students are expected to take a minimum of 3 courses of 2 credits each.

1. Time Management
2. Current Affairs
3. International Relations
4. Indian Constitution
5. Environmental Sociology
6. Legal Literacy
7. Medical Sociology

8. Communication
9. Traditional Indian Systems of Knowledge
10. The Indian Economy
11. Statistical Applications
12. Women's Studies
13. Leadership Effectiveness
14. Economics For Business
15. Human Behaviour
16. Fabric Art
17. Looking at Art
18. Women's Writing
19. History of Ideas
20. Journalism
21. Popular Fiction
22. Advanced Writing Skills
23. Film Appreciation
24. Principles of Accounting
25. Principles of Marketing
26. Principles of Advertising
27. Practical Banking
28. Folklore of Tamil Nadu
29. Tamil Dramatics
30. Public speaking in Tamil
31. Creative Writing in Tamil
32. Spoken Hindi for Beginners
33. Hindi for Advertising
34. Creative Writing in Hindi
35. Public Speaking in Hindi

36. French for Beginners
37. Paintings and Literature of France
38. French for Tourism
39. Upanishads
40. Abhinaya Darpanam
41. Fundamentals of Operations Research
42. Popular Astronomy
43. Everyday Physics
44. Basics of Photography
45. Environment — an overview
46. Chemistry and Society
47. Fruit Preservation
48. Herbal Therapy
49. Everyday Microbiology
50. Human Health and Genetics
51. Music Appreciation
52. Concepts on End User Computing
53. Application Development with DBMS
54. C+ + Programming

CHAPTER 5
VOCATIONALISATION AT THE UNDERGRADUATE LEVEL

A Case Study of H.R. College of Commerce, University of Mumbai in the Vocational Course of Advertising Sales Promotion and Sales.

Management

H.R. College of Commerce and Economics founded in 1960 and affiliated to the University of Mumbai is situated in South Mumbai with an excellent faculty and an intake of bright and talented students.

In 1994 when the UGC introduced the Scheme of Vocationalisation at the First Degree Level, H.R. College was selected for offering Vocational courses in three subjects-

- Advertising, Sales Promotion and Sales Management
- Tax Procedures and Practices
- Tourism and Travel Management

Welcome Change

The introduction of Vocationalisation at the first degree level has indeed been an innovation in the field of higher education. The colleges of the University of Mumbai have taken a lead role in the implementation of the scheme. There has been tremendous enthusiasm on the part of the college staff and students in the introduction of the programme. It is felt that vocationalisation addresses the important issue of relevance of education. There is at present a large gap between education and employment and vocationalisation will help bridge this gap by training students in career oriented courses at the undergraduate level.

In 1994 H.R. College was the college selected by the UGC in the University of Mumbai to offer the vocational course of Advertising Sales Promotion and Sales Management. With 40% growth of advertising industry around the time, the course offered lucrative career options to the students.

Presentations were made to the leading advertising and marketing organizations and agencies about the course and support was enlisted from the industry for resource faculty, on-the-job training and placements. Since its inception many innovative measures have been adopted in implementing the course in the college.

Innovative Measures Adopted in Handling the Issues in Implementation of Vocationalisation

The College experience has shown that despite the initial optimism and enthusiasm from the faculty and students there is growing apprehension of the sustainability of the courses in the future. The programme has entered its fifth year and it is crucial to evaluate its performance in the light of it now being taken over by the State Governments. There have been several issues in the implementation of the courses in H.R. College.

The first and most important issue is of *relevance*. There has been an extensive debate on the direction and content of higher education to cope with the increasing demand of social relevance and employment. In a fast moving global economy the accelerated pace of change demands corresponding changes in academic curriculum. The Vocational Courses have a greater responsibility since they have to cope with the frequent structural and technological changes. The curriculum of Advertising Sales Promotion and Sales Management has been revised within the help of the industry in 1997.

A second important issue is the *financial viability* of these courses after a period of five years when the UGC ceases the funding of the courses. The worry of the Colleges of the University of Mumbai is that in the event of the State Government not supporting these courses financially, the colleges will face a real crunch and be forced to raise funds privately since it may not be possible to charge differential fees which cover the cost of vocationalisation. At present the UGC has estimated an expenditure of over 110 crore rupees to fund the courses for a four year span. The college has developed strong linkages with the industry in the hope that if the State Government does not take up the programme, the industry will support the vocational course.

The most important issue is the administration of the course. Although the vocational curriculum is integrated with the existing core curriculum, the courses require special effort on part of the college administration. Vocationalisation requires the combining of more innovative components with the conventional courses to meet the growing new demands. The co-ordination of guest faculty, evaluation of practical and project work, organization of field visits and liaisons with industry for on- the -job training and placements has increased the administrative burden of the college.

The college in the absence of a co-ordinator has adopted a novel method of co- ordinating it's course. It has appealed to the parents and the user sector to support the course. At present a parent co-ordinator is helping with the administration of the course.

At the heart of any academic programme is the Faculty. An apathetic or an indifferent faculty is a major snag in any educational course.

The competencies of teaching faculty is required in four main directions:

- delivery of a new subject matter which is applied in nature,
- practical training to students in institutions,
- promoting skill development among students which, although carried out with the assistance of personnel of employing establishments with collaboration of the teaching faculty,
- entrepreneurship development.

The advertising course is being taught by the internal faculty and external faculty. A new collaborative model of teaching has been developed for the course.

A New Initiative in Teaching Academia and Industry

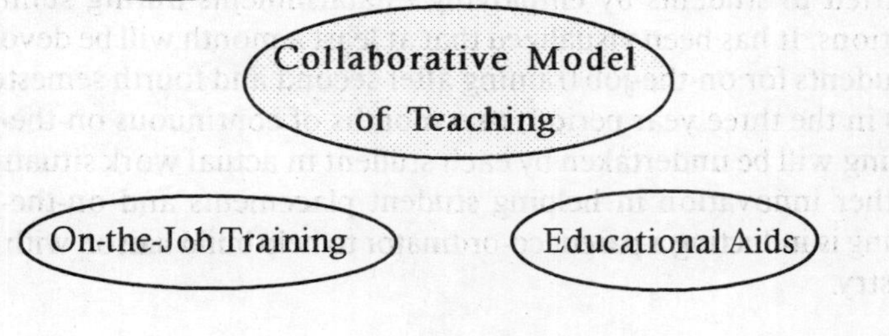

The H.R. College has developed an innovative method of supplementing the internal faculty. The college uses its past students to give guest lectures. The feedback shows that these lectures have been extremely popular and the past students have been able to illustrate their lectures with practical examples from their place of work.

The new professional courses require that the internal faculty be properly trained and qualified in these courses. Upgrading of knowledge and pedagogical skills for teachers is essential. The training work planned by the UGC are insufficient and irregular to cope with the training needs. H.R. College has focused greatly on faculty training. The college has adopted new methods of training the faculty in the subject. These are:

1. Internal faculty sit in on the guest faculty lectures.
2. Internal faculty attend professional seminars, workshop and talks on advertising and marketing.
3. Internal faculty are sent to industry for training.

The selection of students for the courses is of great importance. It was seen that students required vocational counselling to help them make the correct selection of the subject. The process of selection of students in the subject of advertising sales promotion and sales management has been devised by the industry. (Lintas and Hindustan Lever Ltd.) The process consists of:

a) Written Test

b) Group Discussions, and

c) Personal Interviews

An academic cut off percentage is decided and the students are selected on the basis of their creative and other skills and not just on the academic performance.

A key component of vocationalisation is on-the-job training imparted to students by employing establishments during summer vacations. It has been visualized that at least a month will be devoted by students for on-the-job training after second and fourth semesters. Thus in the three year period, two months of continuous on-the-job training will be undertaken by each student in actual work situation. Another innovation in helping student placements and on-the-job training is inducting a parent co-ordinator to help build liaison with the industry.

One of the methods employed by H.R. College to achieve compatible skill development and bring in an awareness of the working life nearer to the student through on-the-job training was to sign memorandum of undertakings (MOU) with the Confederation of Indian Industries (CII) and the Bombay Chambers of Commerce. Presentations were made to the industry on linking organisational adoption of these courses by the employing establishments. The college is making efforts to establish education and business partnerships.

The preconditions of effective integration of such a partnership are -

- Develop a structural relationship
- Industry support should be relevant to the course content
- Identify a champion for the cause
- Industry trainer should be qualified

Project Work

Project work forms an integral part of the vocational courses. Currently 70% of marks are allotted to theory and 30% of the marks to project work at the first year and second year of the programme. In the third year 50% of the marks in one paper are allotted to practical problems and case study.

The project work at all the three years of the vocational programme are handled by *experts* in the *profession.* Projects assigned to students are from the current advertising and marketing scenario are students encouraged to make presentations in front of professionals and parents who are specially invited. This develops *presentation and communication techniques in the students* along with the practical experience of collecting data, undertaking research and creating projects.

The *project workshops* are sponsored by the industry annually and often industry is invited to witness the students' performance for placements. Quite often students are taken out of Mumbai for live projects.

Practical Training

The success of the practical training is evaluated by the learning experienced by the students in the real life of work. In a survey conducted in the college, the responses of 150 senior students on-the-job training were collected. The students were questioned on the method of traning used, on the attitude of the employing organizations and on their learning experience.

The survey revealed the following---

Method of Training used	
Orientation by Supervisor	81%
Through written material	41%
Given a specific project	43%
Orientation by other personnel	55%
Through Observation	70%
Other methods	16%

Attitude of the Employer	
Willing	89%
Not Willing	19%

Learning Experience	
Useful	76%
Relevant to the course	47%
Practical training	93%
Focused on the vocation	26%
Not useful	01%

The practical training was thus considered very useful and relevant to the vocation. However, the students did feel that there were certain constraints faced by them during the hands-on experience at work. Some the of responses were

- One month of training is too short,
- Treated as students, not taken seriously,
- High expectations from the students,
- Unstructured training,
- Students are exploited,
- Not familiar with the in-house culture.

The survey helped the college to understand the problems faced by the students and the employing institutions. As a result, the college made special efforts to help students get the maximum gain out of their on-the-job training.

Some of the measures adopted by the college were

- Orientation of students prior to the training. This was done preferably with the help of employing organizations.
- Liaison between the academic institution and the employing institutions.
- Communication of training objectives to the employing institutions
- Identifying a mentor at both ends
- Visit by the college faculty to the student's place of work
- Detailed report and presentation by the students on the completion of the training
- Evaluation of the student's performance by the employer and the faculty.

Priorities after Graduation

The primary objective of the UGC, State Governments and the Universities in the introduction of these courses was to reduce the gap between education and employment. The courses were intended to be terminal with possibilities of upward mobility for students who wanted to specialized further in the subject. The objectives of vocationalisation at the undergraaduate level were required to ensure.

A study of students graduating in the first and second batches was conducted to determine the priorities after graduation. The study showed that

19%	Graduated were absorbed in jobs related to their vocational subject.
51%	Graduates opted for further studies
30%	Graduates would look for self-employment or join the family business.

In conclusion it can be said that the UGC scheme of Vocationalisation at the Undergraduate level has been a welcome innovation in the higher education scene and a step in the right direction. Implementation of the programme has shown that the effectiveness of the scheme depends on a number of factors which are listed below.

- The capacity of the institutions to run the course in an effective manner and to establish credibility for the programme.

- Linkages with industries and other employing agencies possibly through a Memorandum of Understanding or letter of intent.
- Provide adequate infrastructure both physical and academic.
- Training programmes for faculty.
- On-the-job training for the students offering vocational subjects.
- The production of resource material and support of external resource faculty.
- Active co-operation of the Government, Department of Education and-College engagements.
- Assured supply of funds over an extended period of: 5 to 10 years.
- Amendment of the Apprenticeship Training Act to provide stipends to students of vocational subjects for on-the-job training.

Of the above factors the establishing academia-industry linkages is most crucial in ensuring successful implementation of the scheme of vocationalisation at the first degree level.

RECOMMENDATIONS

The discussion on Curriculum Reforms was initially chaired by Dr. Kaushik and after his departure by Dr. Sr. Annamma Philip.

The discussion began with the group members introducing themselves and briefing the other members of the group on the curriculum reforms that have been introduced in their respective institutions after autonomy was granted.

Dr. G.D. Sharma posed a couple of questions relating to reforms and the idea of flexibility in curricula.

The Following recommendations were made:

1. Empower the teaching community to handle job-oriented and specialised courses.

2. Set up an Academic Staff College exclusively for Faculty of Autonomous Colleges.

3. Permit Autonomous Colleges to organise orientation and refresher courses, keeping in mind the changes, that have become necessary in the curriculum of Autonomous Colleges.

4. Design the curriculum to provide vertical mobility for students as well as to meet changing social needs thus making autonomy the platfom whereby learning becomes a continuous process.

5. Involve several alumni who are employed in different industries/ organisations in the drafting of syllabi.

6. While implementing syllabus the methodology of teaching needs to be spelt out clearly before the course begins.

7. Academic programmes can be conducted as joint ventures between academic institutions and leading industrial organisations.

8. Setting up a Curriculum Development Cell should be made mandatory.

9. Teachers, who are newly appointed in autonomous colleges need to be thoroughly oriented on the philosophy and rationale of autonomy as they take up their teaching assignment.

10. Emphasize on the development of human resource in institutions through various programmes organised for the management, faculty, administrative and support staff students.

Chapter 6
Experience of Field Work

Dr. G. Christopher

I shall report on Field work and various types of projects conducted in Women's Christain College under autonomy and also similar work done in other autonomous colleges.

The Women's Christian College, Chennai was founded in 1915 by the united effort of twelve missionary societies in Britain, Canada and U.S.A. At the beginning the College had only 41 students and 7 faculty members. Today it has grown to approximately 1,100 students and 95 faculty members involved in teaching and administration.

Since 1982, the College has been functioning as an autonomous institution affiliated to the University of Madras. Autonomy gives the College freedom to develop it's curriculum, administer examinations and evaluate the students. From 1994-95 the University Grants Commission has selected the College to offer Vocational Training Courses in Industrial Microbiology and Biotechnology in the Departments of Botany and Zoology respectively.

The curriculum consists of four parts:

Part I is a language course. The College offers three languages namely Tamil, Hindi and French.

Part II is a course in General English.

Part III is the Optional Course. Each student has to choose three courses, one each in the II, III and IV Semesters respectively, the courses being generally from departments other than the one where she is majoring.

Part IV consists of Core and Supporting Courses.

A brief survey of the various field work and projects conducted by the Departments is presented.

Principal, Women's Christian College-600 006

Department of History

Field Work

Field Work is undertaken in the Optional Courses such as Women's Studies, Population Studies and Human Resource Development. Data collected is analyzed and presented as seminars. Seminar topics include subjects like Problems and issues connected with Working Women, Dowry, Changing Attitudes to the Status of Women, Problems of Single Women etc. Other topics include Diseases of Animals in Tamil Nadu, Internet- Worldwide Communication Technology, Female Infanticide and Socio-economic Status of various groups. Work was also done in the Policemen's Quarters in Chennai.

Project Work

The History Department of Women's Christian College introduced a paper in the Core subject for carrying out a project and marked it for 100. The students have to present a research project on topics on institutions, monuments, personalities, industries etc.

From 1992 onwards due to the non-availability of suitable projects within the city, it was decided to have a combined paper of theory for 75 marks and project report of 3000 words for 25 marks. The students concentrated on biographies of personalities. Upto 1996 they covered about 120 personalities. From 1997 onwards, the students do research work for which they are given 40 marks and 60 marks for theory.

Following are the titles of some projects undertaken by the students:

1. Tamil Nadu Fisheries Department- Achievements and Current Projects.
2. Government Museum, Chennai.
3. Manali Petrochemicals, Chennai.
4. Veterinary College, Chennai.
5. Bala Vihar- A Study.
6. Family Planning and Family Welfare Board.
7. Punjab Association and it's units for women.
8. M.S. Subbalakshmi- noted singer of Carnatic Music
9. S. Lakshmi- Author of Tamil Stories.
10. Kapaleeswarar Temple Thirumylai, Chennai.

11. St. Andrews Church Egmore, Chennai.

12. Central Leather Research Institute, Chennai.

13. Study of Diocesan Press, Vepery, Chennai.

14. Growth of the connemara Public Library, Chennai.

15. Bharat Scouts and Guides.

DEPARTMENT PROJECT WORK OF LANGUAGES - TAMIL

In the study of the Tamil Language under autonomy, Tamil Culture and Tamil as medium of instruction were offfered as optional subjects in 1982. For the latter the students collect a science vocabulary of 100 words in English and their corresponding equivalents in Tamil and present topic in a seminar at the end of the semester.

Since 1987 the above topic has been changed to Tamil Culture and Tourism as the former was not so popular with the students. For the Tourism course the students do a project either individually or in groups of two and this is evaluated for 30 marks. Some of the projects undertaken were as follows:

1. Valluvar Kottam
2. Madras Museum
3. Marina & San Thome Cathedral
4. Mahabalipuram
5. Saint Thomas' Mount
6. V.G.P Golden Beach
7. Kancheepuram Temple, all situated in Chennai and Tamil Nadu.

In 1986 Tamil Journalism course was also introduced as an optional subject for which the students submit a project report valued for 30 marks at the end of the semester. In this case the project can be done individually or by two students or as a group of six students. Titles of some projects are:

1. Comparative study of Kumudam & Ananda Vikadsan (Tamil Weeklies)
2. Udavum Karangal-Orphanage-Chennai
3. T.B. Hospital, Chennai
4. Temples such as the one at Tiruvannamalai, Tamil Nadu.

Another project which the students are involved in every year is the publication of a Tamil magazine called Amutha Kalanjiam.

DEPARTMENT OF ENGLISH

Project Work

The projects offered by the Department of English are part of one semester courses open to third year students of B.A., English Literature. The students are trained to do individual work. They are free to choose a research topic from one of the following disciplines:

a) Journalism.

b) Study of Literature (British, American, Commonwealth and Indian)

c) English Language Teaching

d) Advertising

e) Public Relations and

f) Linguistics.

They are taught research methodology and are tested on it. At the end of the semester they are expected to submit a 15 to 30 page dissertation on the topic of their choice.

Journalism : This course is open to B.A. Final Year Literature students and has the following objectives. To understand the impact of the media in particular, the newspaper, on society and to develop skills in reporting, interviewing, writing and editing for a newspaper. The course is designed accordingly. Apart from exercises as classroom activity, a project has been evolved that provides ample opportunity for practical work. The students bring out a monthly campus newspaper called The Rivett. Students are involved in reporting news on campus, in other colleges and in the city, writing features, planning cartoons, puzzles and other fillers for this newspaper. The target audience comprises of the students and faculty of the College. In group, they manage the production of this paper from composition of text to preparation of layouts at Desktop Publishing Centres and procuring revenue through advertisements for the paper. The Rivett project provides scope not only for practical exposure but proves a very satisfying experience for the students as a journalistic effort.

Creative Writing is offered as an optional paper in the IV Semester for the 3 Year degree course. The paper contains units on Features and Articles, Short Story Writing, The Haiku, Writing for Radio and Organizing an Interview.

Group discussion of creative approaches is a method often used in class and is very popular with the students.

The objective of the paper is not only to stimulate the creative curiosity of interested students so that they become more experienced and skilled, but also encourages students to use their creative writing skills for remuneration. The confidence that the students gain from this course can be seen from their successful publishing of material that is submitted for tests or assignments.

Video production and Communication

The B.A. English degree course has a one semester Core paper in Video Production and Communication. The course has the following objectives:

i. To practice Language skills for script writing.

ii. To create awareness of effective visual grammar.

iii. To inculcate a sense of social commitment and responsibility in using video.

Emphasis is placed on the practical work involved in producing a video documentary from research and script-writing to editing. Students are given hands-on training in the use of the video camera. The Department has collaborated with the Film and Television Institute, Chennai, the Technical Teachers Training Institute, Chennai and Dr. Selvam of EMRC, Anna University, Chennai on various aspects of the course. The topics covered by Video production include:

I. Film/Video Analysis and Understanding Visual Language

i. Thematic/Content Analysis.

ii. Structural Analysis.

iii. Cinematographic Analysis

a) Video formats

b) Camera movements and angles

c) Lighting

d) Sound

e) Editing

iv. Moral Ideological Analysis

II. Practical Work

i. Scriptwriting exercises

ii. Exercises in visualization.

iii. Producing a five minute video presentation.

Department of Psychology

Field Work

Every student has a choice of two areas from those listed below and a minimum of five case studies are undertaken by the students.

1. Old Age
2. Problems of Students
3. Learning Disabilities
4. Normal children 3 to 5 years old from a nursery school
5. Delinquents
6. Physically handicapped
7. Mentally Impaired
8. Problems of Women-married, unmarried, widow etc.

The student presents the biography of a person from Data collected from records available from parents and others significant in the subject's life and the individual himself/herself.

The student analyses the behaviour, emotions and beliefs of the single individual in some depth. Suitable recommendations may be offered. This information is submitted in a typed and bound form. This paper is offered to the 3rd year students in the VI Semester and marked out of hundred.

The M.A. Psychology students have been involved in field work at a slum in Adyar and at the T.T. Ranganathan Centre for the Rehabilitation of Alcoholics, Chennai.

Another area of work was the `Study Skills' programme offered to weak students in a Corporation school in Kotturpuram, Chennai.

A Seminar on awareness of `Learning Disabilities' was organized for school teachers in 1998.

Project Work

The M.A. students undergo Internship in the VI Semester. Each student undergoes internship in three institutions for children with mental retardation or other disorders. The student is expected to work in the institution and gain experience in the skills acquired earlier in the classroom. The student is also required to study the structure and the functioning of each institution and make an evaluation. Reports are submitted and evaluated for 75 marks.

In the VI Semester the students carry out case studies and written reports are evaluated for 75 marks. Each student studies three children with mental retardation or other disorders. The student is required to make an assessment, identify problems, plan a therapeutic strategy and make use of at least one intervention technique.

Deapartment of Mathematics

Project Work

The `Future Studies' Optional Course is offered in III Semester for the III Year Degree Course. The student selects a topic based on an issue faced by mankind such as: Terrorism, Nuclear tests, Education, Crime etc. They study the problem from its development to the present situatiion. They also analyse what could happen in the future. They present this in the form of a written project, using newspaper cuttings and statistical data. This is evaluated for 10 marks.

In the course Popular Astronomy the students are allowed to observe celestial objects using the telescope owned by the department. They spend one night on campus and observe the moon, learn to locate stars and planets. By using celestial maps they learn to identify different constellations.

Department of Computer Science

This department started in 1986 offers a balanced combination of hardware and software topics of Computer Science. The students at the fourth semester entering the final year of the degree course are sent for on-the-job training for about 4 to 5 weeks during their summer vacation. They report to companies and institutions which use computers in their routine work. At the end of this period, they submit a report on the work done and are issued a certificate of grading. From such an experience, they learn about the EDP set up, the kind of projects and jobs they can aspire for. The companies that have extended their cooperation are: Ashok Leyland. BHEL, CMDA, CBSI, Harita Finance, Hindustan Photo film,

IGCAR, India Cements, Indian Airlines, Indian Express, Indian Oil Bhavan, Madras Fertilizers, Malai Murasu, Sundaram Information systems, TCS and Wipro Infotech, to name a few.

In the final semester, the students in groups of 2 or 3 take up a project under the direct guidance of the faculty of the department. This paper taken along with 3 other papers in the sixth semester, enables them to consolidate their innovative ideas using any of the latest software like Visual BASIC, Visual C++, FOXPRO, C etc, along with the latest Multimedia facilities. They have developed Computer Aided Learning packages, Application Software and Games projects like: Fractal Fantasy, India-Pre and Post Independence, Language Tutor, Jigsaw Puzzle, College Library Management System, Nutrition and Therapy, Prelude to Piano, Quiz on Network, Snakes and Ladders, Sports etc.

These two components of the course curriculum have enabled many of our graduates to get jobs in reputed companies in India and abroad, students also go in for higher studies in computers and excel.

Department of Physics

Project Work

The Department of Physics offers courses in Photography which are highly job oriented. They are offered at two levels, one for major Physics students and another optional course at the interdepartmental level, Photography is a combination of applied science and arts. Black and white photography and colour photography are featured. The Department has a well equipped Dark room.

The Department of Physics also offers a Vocation oriented course-Work Shop Practice-which is designed to enable students to acquire practical skills in the use of basic workshop machines such as lathes, drilling machines, hand-saw, grinding machines etc. They receive training from qualified technicians and make utility and decorative articles both in wood and metal. B. Sc. Physics Major students design experiments in the workshop to explain principles of physics. The final year students of Physics specializing in Electronics take up individual projects in Electronics of high standard and these projects are generally evaluated by external examiners. The exercise gives them confidence to handle any electronic circuit.

Besides these general projects, interested students take up special projects like microprocessor based audiometer and speech trainer for the hearing impaired funded by external agencies. The successful completion of similar projects places much emphasis on the preparatory work-material research, development of experimental design and fabrication skills and use of statistical methods of analysis. The contact with specialists in the field offers enormous scope for further learning.

Department of Chemistry

Project Work

This faculty undertook a special project on Dyeing and Printing of Textiles under the College Science Improvement Programmes (COSIP). The students were taught methods of dyeing including dyeing with vegetable dyes such as onion skins. Resist printing, in particular Batik was also taught. An examination was held at the end of the year and certificates were awarded to the students. Dr. Miss Parimala Appasamy also brought out a book under the programme titled `A Handbook of Printing and Dyeing of Textiles'.

When the College became autonomous in 1982, Fibres, Fabrics, Dyeing and Printing of Textiles was offered as an optional course which became immensely popular. As part of this course which includes theory (60 marks) the students are taught dyeing with various dyes such as Vat Dyes, Reactive or Procion Dyes, Nylon Dyes, Direct Dyes etc. Different kinds of methods for fabrics such as cotton, wool, silk and nylon are carried out.

Restrict printing to two types: Batik and Tie and Dye form a major part of the course. Batik is taught by a deaf and dumb expert, Mr. Mohan who has, his own Batik Deaf Educational Institute, Chennai. A modified form of this art is practised i.e. after the outline is waxed, the various colours are painted in, then the whole cloth is waxed, dyed, dewaxed and ironed. Tie and Dye was originally taught by an Arts and Handicrafts teacher (Mrs. Meera) but now the faculty are skilled in the different methods used to produce varied effects. The cloth is dyed once or several times according to the number of colours needed.

The students are also taught Block Printing and Screen Printing. The Department has acquired blocks and screens for this purpose. From time to time exhibitions of the work done by the students are held in the College.

Department of Botany

Project Work

In the modified autonomous syllabus group project was introduced for the final year Botany students in the year 1994.

Evaluation is done exclusively by the faculty of the department for 25 marks. The unique features is the planning and the execution of the project. This is then documented and submitted as a project report.

One of the projects was on solid waste management. The solid waste from the college campus such as kitchen waste from the college mess and canteen and litter found on the campus was collected. This was decomposed by vermicomposting by the use of `Farmer's Friends' that is earthworms. A vermit pit laid with bricks, gravel, soil, dung and sand was constructed and the process was carried out in this pit. Samples of the decomposing material were analysed periodically for the microflora with special reference to (a) Total viable count (b) Amylolytic strains (c) Proteolytic strains and (d) Lipolytic strains.

The outcome of the project was rich organic manure which is eco-friendly. Isolates collected from the study provided a rich source of decomposers actively involved in biodegradation and these were preserved on slant cultures for future use.

`On the job' Training was given to the VTC students for 4 weeks at the end of the first and second year. The centres where they are trained are given below:

1. Centre for Advanced studies in Botany, Chennai
2. Central Leather Research Institute, Chennai
3. M.S. Swaminathan Research Foundation, Chennai
4. Murugappa Chettiar Research Centre, Chennai
5. SPIC Science Foundation, Chennai
6. Cancer Research Institute, Chennai
7. Medimix, Chennai
8. Tamilnadu Hospital, Chennai
9. Tamilnadu University of Veterinary and Animal Science,Chennai
10. International Fund for Agriculture Development, Madurai
11. Abraham Pandithar's Herbal and Research Farm, Tanjore
12. Apollo Hospital, New Delhi
13. Valar Thozhil, Chennai
14. Mohan Breweries and Distilleries, Chennai

Field Work

Entrepreneurship

From 1997 in Semester VI the students are offered a course in entrepreneurship. The students are given lectures on how to select the product line, design and development process, economics of materials and energy requirements, stocking the product and releasing the same for marketing. The students are asked to survey the demand for a given product, feasiblity of its production under the given constraints of raw material, energy input, financial implications, export potential etc., procedural details on how to select, process, how to move for loans, how to operate and how to repay the loans in a phasic manner are highlighted during lectures. The students have to give a draft project at the end of the semester.

In the final year the students in group conduct a market survey of household products such as fast foods and cosmetics. The report is submitted at the end of the year which is evaluated for 10 marks.

Department of Zoology

Field Work

Among the project conducted by the Zoology Department in the recent past are:

1. Study of Fauna around the College Campus

The main aim of this project was to make a survey of the fauna found on the campus so that the wide diversity of animal life and their adaptations by which they fit themselves into the environs could be studied taxonomically. The fauna was collected and identified. Different varieties of insects (mainly butterflies and birds) were indentified which were unnoticed until then. What was learnt in the classroom was observed in the natural habitat because of this project.

2. Survey of Socio-Economic Status of Fisher Folk

A Preliminary survey of the indicators of health was conducted in a small fishing village along the seashore in Besant Nagar, Chennai. The survey was conducted over a period of three months during which time an exhaustive study of the living conditions of this community was done. Other areas surveyed are:

a) A comprehensive survey of the health status of the fishermen community by analyzing the various health indices such as socio-economic factors, nutrition, environment, mortality and morbidity and general health indicators in two phases.

b) Information was gathered on the risk factors involved.

c) Suggestions for appropriate measures for the improvement of the health status of this community were given. A household survey was carried out so that 110 families were interviewed.The questionnaire interview method was followed. The survey had provided baseline data with wide coverage for future reference.

3. Biological Control of Mosquito Larvae Using Diplonychus Indicus

The Cocum river which flows adjacent to our College has been an ideal breeding-ground for mosquitos over the years. Various efforts undertaken by the Government to eradicate these vectors have proved futile as the mosquitos have managed to survive and reproduce.

The indiscriminate use of insecticides and pesticides have not only increased respiratory disorders owing to allergy among the human population but has also resulted in the development of resistance of mosquitos and their subsequent outbreaks due to annihilation of their natural predators. These factors have therefore been responsible for evoking considerable interest in the adoption of biological control of the mosquitos. Hence a project on the successful control of the mosquito larvae using the available aquatic bugs was carried out by the students and faculty of Zoology. The aquatic bug, *Diplonychus Indicus* was chosen for this study. The primary aim of the study was to determine the predatory efficiency of D. Indicus on the mosquito larvae (Culex Species) which is abundant in the river Cocum and hence it's potential as a biocontrol agent. The findings had confirmed D. Indicus is a potential biocontrol agent of the mosquito larvae.

Project Work

For on the job training the students had been sent to the following institutes:

1. The Department of Animal Biotechnology-Madras Veterinary College, Chennai.
2. M.S. Swaminathan Foundation, Chennai.
3. Frederick Institute of Plant Protection and Toxicology, Padappai, Tamil Nadu.
4. Department of Cinical Pathology, Tamil Nadu.

5. Good Samaritan Clinical Laboratory, Anna Nagar, Chennai, and
6. Biogene Clinical Laboratory, K.K. Nagar, Chennai.

Department of Home Science

Project Work

Since it's inception in the 1950s, the Home Science Department has done pioneering research and field work mainly in the area of Foods and Nutrition besides Food Service Management and Extension activities. They have published their findings in well known journals and addressed many forums in the city and at the national and international level.

In the area of Foods and Nutrition they have not only done innovative work but also tried to meet felt needs of the city and the state. To mention a few, the success of the Chief Minister's Nutritious Noon Meal Programme has been tested by the biochemical as well as anthropometric measurements and it was found that it was beneficial to the health of the children. The use of indigenous cheaper cereals such as Amaranthus and the iron rich Sundakkai and other low cost food freely available in the market was advocated after testing the increase in weight and other indicators of good health on volunteers such as students of various age groups in the city school and elsewhere. Studies were carried out on the nutritional requirements of pregnant women, adolescent girls and other age groups, status of clinical Nutrition such as diabetes, diarrhoea, cancer etc.

The prevalence of iodine deficiency disorders among school children (10-19 years) in Chennai and in rural areas were some of the projects undertaken. The use of supplements like iron fortified salt on the health of the hostel student of WCC was studied and had illuminating results.

Feeding trials have been carried out on albino rats and human volunteers to evaluate the nutritional qualities and therapeutic effect of 'Spirulina'.

Many of these studies were conducted by the students especially the postgraduates under the guidance of faculty mambers, other were by the faculty and still others were carried out by the undergraduate students also.

A number of projects in the use of audio-visual material for extension work and the use of folk arts in non-formal teaching were carried out and found to be very effective.

Some of the other areas of Research include:

1. Role of oils in lowering blood cholesterol.
2. Herbs in the management of Diabetes Mellitus.
3. Impact of cereal pulse mixtures in lowering blood glucose levels, and
4. Trials on the use of Arugampillu, Kizhanelle etc. in control of Diabetes and Cholesterol levels.

Feild Work

The postgraduates students also conduct studies on community nutrition as part of their field work. They live in a rural area for a while and study the nutritional status of the villages by questionnaire as well as by weighment method, Anthropometric measurements, conducting food and nutrition surveys on selected groups. They plan and conduct and evaluate nutrition and educational programmes. Based in their findings they advocate superior nutritional substitutes which are at the same time economical.

Catering and Internship

The M.Sc. Food Service Management and Dietetics students have to undergo work experience for 4 week period in a well established catering institution such as the Dietary Department Christian Medical College Hospital, Vellore.

Other Autonomous Colleges

1. *P.S.G. College of Technology-Coimbatore* conducts three internal tests for a course. Out of the three tests one may be a seminar/technical paper/mini project.
2. *Government Arts College-Coimbatore* conducts a vocational course in economics called Advertising and Sales Management. The students undergo job training in Advertising, Sales promotion and entrepreneurship development and submit project work for the completion of the course.
3. *Coimbatore Institute of Technology* has project work as part of the curriculum. These projects are relevant to industries and also include the latest developments in the respective chosen field. The students of all branches of study (UG/PG) utilise the facilities of Computer Aided Design (CAD) centre of instruction for their project work or dissertation.

Field Work

The students are encouraged to undergo Field training/Vocation training/Inplant training for a minimum duration of 6 weeks with a view to prepare and acclimatize themselves to the environment of the industries.

4. *Gobi Rural Arts & Science College* has introduced project work in the curriculum for Computer Science, Management, Economics, Mathematics and Commerce courses.

5. *Sri G. V.G. Visalakshi College for Women, Udumalpet* conducts assessment of feasibility reports prepared based on the study of Small Scale/Rural Industries for a period of 15 days for UG/PG students in lieu of the third internal test (25 marks and 30 marks) respectively. The students have undertaken a project 'Save the Book' using the NSS volunteers for clothing the books with polythene wrappers.

For enhancing the vocabulary and communicative abilities of students, the English department has its own publications.

The Departments of Physics and Zoology through networking facilities and services of the laboratories have a 'Health Centre' to create awareness about health through maintaining basic health information like weight, BP, Haemoglobin, Glucose level, ECG, Urea level etc.

6. *St. Joseph's College, Tiruchirapalli* in order in achieve excellence has upgraded the syllabi for all courses for UG/PG classes. Project work has been introduced as integral part of each course in the last semester for all disciplines.

Field Work

The college has introduced a life-oriented educational programme for all students which will provide opportunities for young men and women to experience the living conditions of the rural poor and arouse in them a genuine desire to serve them and to acquire a sense of discipline and team work. This extension service programme is called 'Science and Humanities for People's Development-The Shepherd programme'. This programme envisages the students and their teachers of various discipline trying to use their knowledge in backward and rural areas approaching the people as learners and not as teachers and assisting them to develop themselves making use of available resources. Each PG student has to put in minimum of 80 hrs service under this programme: 20 hrs of seminars and 40 hrs of contact with the people- all spread over 2 semesters. Each U.G. student has to put in a minimum of 100 hrs of service under this programme. 20 hrs of camp experience, 30 hrs of theory and 50 hrs of contact with the people all spread over 4 semesters. This is obligatory for obtaining the degree.

7. AVC *college-Mayilalduthurai* has group projects and individual projects with viva-voce for UG & PG Students.

8. *Seethalakshmi Ramaswami College Tiruchirapalli* - All postgraduation courses have projects in the final semester of the curriculum and there is tie up with industries like IGCAR, BHEL, CECRI etc.

9. *In Madras Christian College , Tambaram, Chennai* project report and field work constitute compulsory components of evaluation.

10. *Stella Maris College,* Chennai adopted various projects to sensitize the students to social realities and make them agents of social change. Special mention is made of the Functional Literacy Programme and the culture and drug abuse project. The setting up of a writing centre at Stella Maris a project conceived for and involving the UG students of the college, has added an innovative dimension of the teaching and writing skills in English to students.

11. *Sacred Heart College,* Thirupattur has a variety of extension programmes which have been introduced. Of these the BIRD project (Bosco Integrated Rural Development project) is important. The aim of this project is preparing the students to become socially conscious and assume responsibility as agents of social change.

12. *Loyola College* : Besides the conventional methods of teaching like lectures, students participation is recognized and encouraged through seminars, project work, assignments etc. Evaluation is based on continuous internal assessment and end of semester examination with equal weightage for each. Continuous assessment comprises scheduled tests and particularly assignments, quizzes, projects and case studies.

13. *Queen Mary's College* : To improve skills the projects report writing is introduced at PG level which includes viva-voce assessments.

14. *Sri Sarada College for Women, Salem* gives more emphasis on field work and on-the-job training under autonomous pattern.

15. *Ayya Nadar Janakiammal College, Sivakasi* has project work which is compulsory for postgraduate students.

16. *Thitagarajah College of Engineering, Madurai* : Miniprojects are done in their projet work.

17. *Thiyagarajah College, Madurai.* Field work and project work are specialities for them. The students are given uptodate training by the industrial companies and they are to do projects with novel innovations and ideas, however small they may be. Teachers insist that their project work must necessarily have a computer based component.

18. *The Fatima College, Madurai.* Project work and field work introduced under autonomy.

19. *The American College, Madurai.* Students are given opportunity to do field work and are taken on study tours to learn beyond the classroom.

20. *Lady Doak College, Madurai.* Field work is conducted under Women's studies. Project work is evaluated from the final report and viva-voce.

21. *G.T.N. Arts College, Dindigul*: The Department of Physics provides a paper for 100 marks on project and field visits for the final year B.Sc. Physics students.

22. *Madura College,* Self learning is motivated and encouraged. Project work is a component of the programme of most of the departments.

23. *St. Xavier's College, Palayamkottai.* Student Training and Action for Neighbourhood Development - The modern emphasis of taking University Education to the village so that the poor of the rural area may benefit from the fruits of research, teaching and learning in the institution is the sole aim of this pioneering outreach, programme STAND introduced in the academic year 1993-94. The primary objectives of this programme is to contribute to the total development of people through awareness and training. In the students, it aims at creating a sense of social justice and social concern through exposure to rural realities leading to a committed involvement towards the integrated development of the rural poor. This is a compulsory programme in which all year UG and first year PG students are required to participate. A fee of Rs. 50/- is collected from each student at the beginning of the 1 year for incidental and travel expenses for the entire year.

Every department will be allotted one village around Palayamkottai within a radius of 20 to 25 Kms. After an orientation programme of theory and practical field experience, the students will be required to visit their `adopted' villages and interact with the people at regular intervals. This involvement and exposure, under the guidance of staff, will make their learning, socially relevant and useful both to the villagers and to the students. Each department will have one member of the staff as contact person to whom the students could refer matters that concern this village programme. The main activities that will be taken up by STAND are : (1) Environment (2) Literacy (3) Health and Nutrition (4) Helping the villagers to solve basic problems like drinking water, electricity, transport, patta for housing, road-laying etc., by contacting Government and voluntary agencies.

The 100 hrs required for the courses will be divided into the following components : 30 hrs theory (foundation courses) for UG students, (Seminar) for PG students, 10 hrs field experience, 60 hrs of village development work.

24. *Sri Parasakthi College for women, Kuttralam.* Individual project work, submission of thesis and viva-voce for PG students individual/group wise project for UG are compulsory and evaluation for UG project is purely internal.

25. *C.H.S.D. St. Theresa's Autonomous College for Women, West Godavari District* has introduced a project study (a mini dissertation) in the Vth semester for all the final year students. Reference, interview, questionnaire, consolidation, drafting etc. are part of project study by the students.

26. *M.R. College, Vizianagaram (A.P.).* Students actively participate in certain restructured courses such as Rural Industrialization and Management studies taking into consideration the rural background of the local area. Students are attracted to these courses. Educational tours and Field work are arranged as part of class work for certain courses - social work, IRPM etc., Project work, on the job training is also provided in courses such as Electronic Equipment Maintenance.

27. *St. Joseph's College for Women, Visakkapatanam (A.P.).* Minor project work in all Science and Arts subjects has been introduced whereas in some subjects Major Project work replaces a theory paper.

28. *Anwarul Uloom College, Osmania University.* It is proposed to make project work compulsory so that the student acquires knowledge of practical application and it will help them to find jobs on completion of the degree. For example, the students of Computer Science will be asked to work on some real life practical projects.

29. *St. Francis College for Women, Hyderabad, Osmania University.*

Every student is involved in at least one miniproject. The B. Com. professional students have project work as one of the papers.

Conclusion

I have drawn the following conclusions from these :

- Project and Field work promote a higher standard and level of achievement.
- It prepares the students for higher studies.
- As the students work in various organizations and industries, they learn not only the technical aspects but also build a rapport with the outside world and it will increase their eagerness for achieving academic excellence.
- The students acquire knowledge of the problems involved and how to solve them.
- By engaging in Field work the students work shoulder to shoulder with the less privileged and rural poor and so learn about poverty and development in India.

CHAPTER 7
FIELD AND PROJECT WORK IN AUTONOMOUS COLLEGES

A.L. Mohan*

1. SDS Autonomous College had the uniqe distinction of offering 3 year B. Sc. courses with Mineral Beneficiation, Geology and Materials Handling/Chemistry as optional subjects since 1977. It also had the distinction of being the first Autonomous College in the country to offer 3 year B.Sc. course with Geo-Exploration and Drilling Technology, Mathematics and Physics under the UGC scheme of vocationalisation of undergraduate courses.

2. Consequent to the grant of Autonomous status to this College in 1987, it became possible to revamp the syllabi in the subjects of the above referred courses, meeting the needs of the possible employer through interaction with the experts from the relevant industries (private and public undertakings).

3. In order to ensure employability, it became necessary to incorporate practical training for the students (by way of project work and field study) for acquiring contemporary skills in their fields of study.

Former Principal, SDS Autonomous College, Shreeramnagar-535101

[In Collaboration with D.V. Subba Rao, HOD, Mineral Benefication, SDS Autonomous College, Shreeramnagar - 535 101, Andhra Pradesh]

4. Thus the students of the above referred courses in groups (each group consisting of two or three students), were compulsorily deputed for practical training for a period of 4 weeks at the end of fourth semester to the following organisations.

1. National Metallurgical Laboratory, Jamshedpur and Chennai.
2. Regional Research Laboratories, Bhopal and Bhubaneswar.

Former Principal, SDS Autonomous College, Shreeramnagar-535101
[In Collaboration with D.V. Subba Rao, HOD, Mineral Benefication, SDS Autonomous College, Shreeramnagar - 535 101, Andhra Pradesh]

3. Atomic Minerals Division, Hyderabad.
4. National Mineral Development Corporation, Hyderabad.
5. Indian Bureau of Mines, Nagpur.
6. Manganese Ore (India) Limited, Nagpur.
7. Salgaocar Mining Industries Limited, Margoa.
8. Sociedade de Fomento Industrial Limited, Margoa.
9. Essar Pellatisation Plant, Visakhapatnam.
10. Ore Handling Complex, Visakhapatnam.
11. Mineral Exploratiion Corporation, Nagpur.
12. National Drilling Centre, Nagpur.
13. Oil and Natural Gas Commission, Rajahmundry.
14. Geological Survey of India, Hyderabad.

5. Prior to attending the practical training they are given orientation in the subjects (Mineral Beneficiation, Materials Handing and Geo-exploration and Drilling Technology) and familiarise them with the machinery (operating models being available in the college laboratory) on which they would be having hands-on experience during the practical training.

6. During their practical training at various organisations, each student was given a problem for investigatiion, using their theoretical knowledge. On the basis of the submission of their investigation, the organisation gave participation certificates. The students attended the practical training at their own cost and were not awarded any marks for this. Thus it was in addition to normal prescribed curriculum and benefitted them in getting placement in relevant fields.

7. In the subject of Geology, the students were sent on field study which was a part of the prescribed curriculum for visiting sites of geological importance and made to submit a report on their visit for which scores were awarded forming a part of the internal assessment component.

In addition, the volunteers of NSS unit of the college under the guidance of the faculty members of the department of Geology are exposed to the methods of exploring ground water resources and soil testing in the villages nearby. (This is taken as an additioinal input of their learning without being considered for securing marks).

8. One of the alumni of SDS Autonomous College, Mr. Vijaya Kumar P. was the recipient of National Metallurgist Young Scientist Award of Indian Institute of Metals for 1996 for his outstanding research in Metallurgy.

9. The paper prepared by Mr. Vijay D and Mr. K. Venkataraju (during their period of study of the B.Sc. course) ``Pelletisation of Iron Ores" was accepted and presented in CHESS-95 of Siddaganga Institute of Technology, Tumkur.

II

Whatever that goes in the name of project work or field study (in many subjects) is mostly hackneyed and does not enhance the marketability of the graduates. It is therefore suggested that the following issues on the subject be taken up for a dispassionate and thorough discussion in this workshop and formulate guidelines for implementing them in the 21st century.

- Project Work and Field study (by whichever suitable alternative name they could be called) must be made a part of the curriculum.

- It should be done by not more than three students and they be made to give a presentation which shall be evaluated by the teachers and his co-students and given a score that should form a component of the internal assessment.

- The aim and objectives of Project work/Field study must be clearly enunciated and they must help the students to acquire skills improving their employability.

- It is possible to identify areas for such work only by interacting with the experts from organisations/industries/institutions etc. situated in the vicinity of the college.

- It is high time that we give up the prevalent archaic way of presenting such project reports or field study and ensure that they are bereft of unnecessary, avoidable, showcasing of such reports/studies.

RECOMMENDATIONS
EXPERIENCE OF FIELD VISITS AND PROJECT WORK

Prof. H.P. Dixit, Bhuj University, M.P.

The 15 member group was presided over by the Vice Chancellor of Bhuj University and had the benefit of several experts, viz. from NIEPA, Department of Higher Education in State Governments and the General Secretary of AIFUCTO.

Group discussion was focussed on the following issues :

1) Linking curriculum with the field work/project work.

2) Difficulties encountered in implementing autonomy .

3) Identification of the types of field work/projects.

The following recommendations were made-

1. Whenever project involving field experiences or even simple research is included in the curriculum, the system of its grading and implementation must be clearly defined for ensuring the credibility of its evaluation.

2. In case project/field work is undertaken as part of extension work, which is supposedly supplementary to the main curriculum, sustained participation of students should be mandatory for the sake of continuity and effective production of appreciable results in the target group/ community.

3. Whenever field work or a project is undertaken with a job orientation, or is meant to be need-based, or is relevant to local requirements, all infrastructural facilities and available expertise be utilized both in the project itself and in the form of a consultancy group.

4. Mini projects of shorter duration with identified groups of students may be initiated in collaboration with the local user agencies.

5. The group felt very strongly about all colleges having an inbuilt system

of field/project work for job orientation for extension of classroom learning to field experiences as community outreach activity. In the case of autonomous colleges this should be made an obligatory practice.

CHAPTER 8
EXAMINATIONS - LOYOLA COLLEGE EXPERIMENT

V. Joseph Xavier

A. Semester

As an autonomous college, Loyola has adopted the semester-cum-credit system. The courses consist of core, allied, optional and general elective subjects.

B.Credits

Each course offered in a semester is assigned a certain number of credits depending upon the quantum of work required for the subject. This work consists of lectures, tutorials, seminars, laboratory work, directed library work, etc. For example, a 3 credit course will normally involve 3 hours of lecture and an appropriate amount of tutorials, etc. per week. In science courses, 2 hours of laboratory work per week will generally be given 1 credit. Some non-academic courses like NSS, CSS, Sports, Rotaract, AICUF are given 3 credits. It is a must for a degree. To get a UG & PG degree, 106 and 60-70 are needed.

C.Evaluation

The college has adopted the system of evaluation based both on continous assessment and terminal examinations. Equal weightage (50%) will be given to continuous and termimal assessments. The continuous assesement, will be through announced tests, assignments, seminar and group discussion, snap-test laboratory work, project etc. The student's regularity as indicated by attendance will also be taken into consideration for continuous assessment.

Terminal assessment will be in the form of comprehensive written examination for each course at the end of the semester. The academic year onwards (Nov. 98) we have internal setting for both UG and PG. The

Question Papers will be scrutinised by a board. The board for UG consists of the Head and the senior most member of the department, and one more permanent member of the department; the third member will be appointed on rotation every year. The board for PG consists of the Head and the senior most member of the department and the two external members.

We have for both UG and PG double valuation. The examiners come together and value separately and consolidate the results.

The minimum pass for UG and PG is as follows :

	C.A.	Terminal	Aggregate
U.G.	....	35%	40%
P.G.	....	45%	50%

N.B. a) There is no minimum for C.A.

b) C.A. and Terminal exams. marks are taken together for an aggregate.

There is no restriction on the number of times a failed candidate may appear for a particular paper. However, he will be permitted to retake the paper under the same regulations in the two immediate successive examinations only. After that he will have to repeat the examination under the existing regulations.

Appeals regarding Internal Assessment

Any student who has any grievance regarding continuous assessment may bring it to the notice of the teacher concerned within one week after the receipt of the answer script. If he still feels aggrieved, he can represent the matter to the Head of the Department. After that he may appeal to the Principal who will set up a Committee consisting of two external professors and the Head of the Department. The decision of the Committee will be final. Representations regarding continuous assessment should be made before the end of the semester concerned.

Representation regardig Terminal Examinations results

Representations regarding any corrections, Re-totalling of the results of the terminal examinations must be made to the Controller of Examinations within the time limits prescribed. There is no revaluation under this double valuation system.

Conducting Examinations

For the continuous assessment, the question papers are set by the course teacher and they are prepared by the Controller's Office.

There are two internal tests in a semester.

The Controller's Office prepares the question paper for terminal examination and the college appoints the Chief Superintendent who conducts the semester examination. There are no external invigilators for the semester examination.

The Difference Between University and Autonomous College

University	Autonomous College
a) Semester is optional	a) Obligatory
b) There is no credit system	b) Credit system is followed
c) Sufficient credits are not a condition for promotion	c) Minimum credits of 12 is required for promotion to next year
d) Attendance 75 to write the University Examination. Less than that, condonation fee is collected	d) The same procedure is followed
e) For U.G. there is one valuation only	e) Double valuation both for UG and PG
f) Continuous Assessment is not obligatory	f) Continuous Assessment is compulsory, however , there is no minimum for C.A. But for terminal 18/50 for U.G. & 23/50 for P.G. is compulsory

RECOMMENDATIONS

Examination and Evaluation

This group alone consisted of the largest segment of the conference and, therefore the issue of examination and evaluation was discussed in two separate sub-groups with different chairpersons and rapporteurs. However, the report which follows is joint and covers all aspects of the issue.

The group emphasized the fact that an acceptable system of examination/evaluation must necessarily possess identifiable characteristics like the following :

1) social credibility

2) transparency

3) ability of assessing not only the knowledge/information content but also the skills and values.

4) inherent possibility of bias-elimination and proof against mal practice

The group discussed the practice of over-emphasizing 'writing' in all forms of examination/evaluation. Alternatives to 'writing' may also be considered for the development of students, multi-faceted personality, such as viva-voce, group discussion, quiz, seminars, paper presentation, field trips and project work. Qualities like leadership, sociability, cooperation, discipline, value-based living require distinctly different forms of evaluation than mere 'writing' of examination papers.

In this regard, the group identified three major aspects of examination :

1) pattern of examination

2) its conduct

3) evaluation

While 100% internal examination should remain the ideal to be achieved, there is a need to determine the ratio between classroom instruction and evaluation. The ideal may be 75% and 25% respectively.

Transparency involves an aggrieved student being able to compare his/her own script with that of any other student of his/her choice. Also there should be a way to evaluate/test concept formation/understanding in place of the current practice of judging the quality and quantum of memorisation and written scripts.

The group also noted that since no fool-proof method of examination is possible because all systems have been found to suffer from one or the other inadequacies, individual institutions should evolve it themselves. While teacher themselves need periodic orientation in this area, alternatives to written examination should also be tried. The group wanted teachers to develop a positive attitude toward evaluation. Matters could decidedly be improved if question banks start working and Grievance Cells came into existence in all institutions.

The group also wanted UGC's regional offices to start becoming centres of friendly guidance and help. Other centres may also develop question banks the way the Southern Regional Office has gone about doing the job.

There was a need for introducing a periodic academic audit to increase the credibility of examinations.

For developing a continuous internal assessment system, the group suggested a model examination be conducted before the students appear in the terminal examination. It was emphasized that a good evaluation is one which is both continuous and internal with the following weightages.

i)	Monthly one hour tests (2best out of 3)	10%
ii)	Seminars / Workshops	5%
iii)	Project Wok / Assignment	5%
iv)	Model Examination	30%
v)	Terminal Examination	50%
	Total	100%

Besides the format of the question paper which may include questions requiring long answers, short/very short answers or one out of multiple choices. students should be assessed for their reasoning power and the ability to convert information into its application.

The recommendations were made on the assumption that appropriate modification needed to be applied as and when required.

Chapter 9
Autonomous Colleges - Problems and Prospects

Prof. Mrinmoy Bhattacharyya
General Secretary, AIFUCTO

The satellite system of higher education with an affiliating university and many affiliated colleges which we inherited from the British rule in our country is more in the nature of an exception or aberration by international comparison. In our country, the system started with the establishment of Calcutta University, while the other two universities in Bombay and Madras established in the same year - 1857, were structurally campus universities. Calcutta University was granted jurisdiction over the entire British empire, east of Suez canal. All institutions of higher education in the far-flung empire were affiliated to it. At that time secondary education leading to matriculation was also under universities. All recognised secondary schools also were under the jurisdiction of Calcutta University. Gradually new universities were set up. Many of them followed the pattern of Calcutta University, Bombay and Madras universities also became affiliating universities each with a large number of colleges. At the same time some other universities like Allahabad, Aligarh and Banaras Hindu University were established without any affiliated colleges. Later on, "Boards of secondary education and intermediate and higher secondary education" were set up to relieve the burden of affiliating universities. Thus the present state of affairs evolved gradually responding to the needs and claims of the society. Proliferation of colleges, most of them without any financial aid from the government, which is a recent phenomennon in states like Bihar, Orissa, Assam and Andhra Pradesh has made the system crowded and unhealthy.

Satellite system had a lot of inherent problems besides which there were circumstantial and temporary problems.

Earlier presented at a seminar held on the occasion of XXI annual academic conference of AIFUCTO in Calcutta on 1-3 November'98.

Following are the problems of the first category :

1. Colleges are non-uniform in size of staff, students, academic infrastructure, quality of management and academic performance. But they are treated at par by the affiliating university. Equal treatment of unequals is an act of injustice.

2. Higher education is basically pursuit of excellence. Excellence by definition is available to a few and this deserves and requires special nature and support. In the satellite system this becomes difficult.

3. In a dynamic economy and society many courses require abandonment. Similarly, newer disciplines and courses have to be started. Many of these new courses may again have to be given up or substantially modified very soon. In a satellite system such experimentation becomes difficult.

4. In a satellite system the evaluation is done through common public examination. While anonymity in it has its advantages of impartiality and surprise, the disadvantages are also many. The most prominent being the chance element. Reliability of examination becomes low when examinees do not have a chance to challenge the results. In a big affiliating university, to allow this questioning and re-examination; creates serious practical problems.

5. In the affiliating system the bulk of college teachers practically enjoy very little academic authority. They also do not enjoy real academic freedom in terms of taking decisions to frame courses or to make experiments in teaching methology. Entire teaching-learning process in such a system, is dominated by the public examination system.

All these are old problems and have been debated over decades. For the first time Education Commission (64-66) in its report recommended granting autonomy to some colleges, or some groups of colleges which have shown exceptionally good performance. The report made certain suggestions regarding what may constitute the criteria of goodness of performance. It also suggested that such autonomy should not be permanent in nature.

The idea did not get much support among political authorities as well as the academics. However, some state governments, the lead being given by Tamil Nadu, started this experiment.

In 1986, with the publication of "Challenge of Education" the idea of autonomous colleges got a new boost. By that time the central government and also the UGC came to believe that there were already many colleges in the country and the task was to close down many such colleges.[1] There were suggestions to convert many of them into community polytechnics. The perspective was to grant autonomy gradually to all colleges and finally make them independent universities. Students passing out from such institutions would be known by the names of these institutions. Since employers will be discriminating, only such institutions gradually will be able to attract adequate number of students, whose performance is satisfactory. Others not so-good institutions will have a natural death. Thus autonomous college scheme was viewed as the principal mechanism : (i) to weed out weak and bad colleges, (ii) to ensure enhancement of quality, and (iii) to put an end to the systemt of affiliated colleges.

It is interesting that there was no talk of putting an end to proliferation of colleges, which AIFUCTO demanded. We demanded that the UGC Act may be amended to substitute university by institutions of higher education which should be allowed to be established only by legislation either by Parliament or by State Assembly. We made representations to successive Prime Ministers and Union Education Ministers as well as education ministers from different states. But our representations have gone in vain, and proliferation of colleges, most of them unaided, has continued.

In 1986-87, AIFUCTO firmly opposed the scheme of autonomous colleges for various reasons. It could not be a party to the mass carnage of colleges and their teachers and non-teaching staff serving therein. The scheme was also opposed by the state governments as well as universities for different reasons.

The experiment of autonomous colleges was welcomed primarily by some strongly entrenched private managements, many of them were already enjoying constitutional protection. Their main interest was to be able to run their colleges as their fiefdom. One major attraction to join the scheme was the offer of an alluring grant from the UGC.

Criticism of AIFUCTO against the autonomous college scheme were based on following counts:

1. If the best colleges of university are granted autonomy, they practically go out of the university. Thus the university is left with only not so good colleges, and its products vis-a-vis those of autonomous colleges may lose goodwill of society.

2. Highly meritorious students from small non-autonomous colleges now have a chance to out-compete all the students from the better known

colleges and get recognition. This chance may get lost.

3. The same is true for the best students of autonomous colleges. We were told by students when we visited such colleges that, they would like to be the best not only in their own colleges but in the whole university. This chance is lost.

4. As the courses and examinations will be executed internally, this will make them unreliable. Reliability of marking may also not be above doubts.

5. Teachers will be engaged in a host of routine clerical work. Adequate support of auxiliary staff may not be available.

6. Pressure from authorities, students and their guardians on teachers may be formidable. They are also likely to be penalised if the students do not perform well for no fault of theirs.

7. Students on the other hand complain of being harassed and threatened by teachers because of internal decision making. It is interesting to note that hardly any student wants to continue P.G. studies in an autonomous college if he/she can get a chance to study in the university department.

8. In most of these institutions, teachers do not enjoy freedom to have their unions.

9. Experiment in new courses today is generally marginal or cosmetic in nature.

Positive points of the Scheme

1. Appraisal of performance of colleges is necessary if we want to improve their functioning. Treating the best and worst alike is unjust. The best should get recognition and special support. Autonomous status ensures that.

2. An already good college, if granted autonomy can perform wonderfully well.

3. A good autonomous college can make suitable changes in formulating courses and curricula and promptly responds to the needs of locality and time.

4. Intensity of work in an autonomous college is pronounced. Thus an average teacher has to and does much more work and does it also better.

5. The urge to seek recognition as a good teacher in a good institution ensures the sense of institutional belonging or even loyalty. This is also

true for students. Loss of anonymity of a big university system thus provides better scope and urge for improvement.

6. Unnecessary loss of teaching days in publication of examination result is minimised. Thus number of working days is unusually more in autonomous colleges.

7. Colleges which can aspire to be deemed universities, may be granted autonomy since it can act as a probationary period for the same.

In any case in the foreseeable future the system of affiliated colleges and the satellite system of autonomous colleges, removing the shortcomings of its present structure may be tried in only the very best of the colleges for allowing them to function even better. We should recognise that higher education requires judicious discrimination in the pursuit of excellence and the basic purpose of autonomous college is just that.

Chapter 10
Problems of Administration and Finance and College-University-State Government-UGC Relationship

DR. S. John Britto, S.J.*

IT is interesting to note that all well-documented accounts of autonomous colleges in our country, starting with the Kothari Commission Report through the Malcolm Adiseshiah's statement on autonomous colleges, while being very elaborate on the necessity and the aims of the autonomous colleges are relatively speaking reticent about the financial back-up and even more so on the administrative skills and measures for the successful conduct of these institutions. There is a heavy insistence on excellence, innovation and transpatency in various aspects of the curricular programmes of the institutions which to be merely implemented, leave alone being implemented efficiently, requires a fairly elaborate infrastructure in terms of human resources and equipment. It seems lop-sided to pile up platitudinous statements on what should be done to make the concept of autonomy serve the real needs of education in our country, while taking for granted that the existing pattern of funding and the promises made by the UGC and the state governments will be sufficient to turn the concept of autonomy into a reality.

At stake is the necessity of the autonomous colleges to maintain the unfettered freedom of human mind to apply its powers and methods of reason. It calls for a disciplined, rigorous, relentlessly unprejudiced testing of ideas against observable reality. Such an endeavour is totally dependent on the establishment of standards for the conduct of work and the selection of participants' managerial, teaching and studying on the right lines. In other words, every autonomous college is a potential innovative organisation. In this context, it is very advantageous to associate a college with an organisation, since it will focus our attention on the wherewithals to run an organisation/institution rather than cruise

Principal, St. Joseph's College (Autonomous), Tiruchirapalli-620 002. Tamil Nadu at the dizzy heights of conceptual configurations of what constitutes education. Peter F. Drucker says that the innovative strategy assumes that "whatever exists is ageing and will have to be changed or replaced" by not with something that is "Better and More" but with that is "New and Different" and to achieve this we require "different measurements and a different use of budgets and budgetary controls from those appropriate to an ongoing business." It is significant to note that financial support is as important as ideas are in any enterprise. Since an autonomous college by definition is allowed to have its "self norms", it is essential to ensure that the support financial and statutory—from the UGC, the state government and the parent university is given to the college in such a manner that its objective is in no way destroyed or compromised. The several provisions that are attached to the description of autonomy and the dependence of these institutions on the UGC and the State Governments for financial support and the parent university for accreditation of the curriculum are too well known in depicting the predicament of these colleges in our country.

Aggravating the already precarious position of the autonomous colleges is the discussion paper on "Government Subsidies in India" issued by the Government of India in May 1997. The paper states that the subsidy for services provided in 1994-95, by Central and State Governments was 14.4% of the GDP and there was a need to cut it by 50 per cent. To do so, it distinguishes between 'merit' and 'non-merit' subsidies based on the 'externalities' associated with goods/services. Surprisingly, education other than elementary and agricultural education has been brought under the category of 'non-merit' service[1], because the benefits of subsidies accrue primarily to the recipients. On subsidies to higher education the paper says:

Most subsidies to higher education accrue predominantly to the better-off sections of society and they have an overwhelming advantage in competing out perspective candidates from the other sections in getting admission to courses that are characterised by scarcity of seats.... A significant portion of susbsidies in higher education is appropriated by the middle to high income groups, because shortages of seats in these sectors are cleared by quality-based cleaning in the shape of entrance examination, interview, group discussion etc. Where the poorer sections of society are easily competed out... it may not be unreasonable to set a target of reducing subsidy for non-merit subsidies from 90% to50 % in three years, with a further goal of reducing it to 25% in another two years.

The policy has since been reviewed. Editor

In a brilliant critique of the governments position Prof. K B Powar in his article entitled 'Government Support for Higher Education' has exposed the prejudiced view of the government by tracing it to the current thinking of the World Bank as enunciated by George Psacharapolous and to the disregard of the recommendations of the Punnayya Committee (UGC, 1993) and the Pylee Committee (UGC, 1997). On the other hand the UNESCO policy paper, 'Document of Policies for the Change and Development of Higher Education' (UNESCO, 1995) states that the "State and Society must perceive higher education not as a burden on federal budgets but as a long term domestic investment, in order to increase economic competitiveness, cultural development and social cohesion."It is strange that the current thinking of the government should consider investment in higher education will not contribute to the growth of the economy. Prof. K B Powar after a logical presentation of the unreasonableness of the government's assumption forcefully concludes:

The bottom-line is that the government cannot afford to abruptly withdraw support to higher education as proposed in the discussion paper 'Government Subsidies in India' circulated by the Department of Economic Affairs, Ministry of Finance. Such a step will have a detrimental effect on socio-economic development and on national identity, it is necessary that government continues to shoulder the major responsibility as regards funding of higher education.

Strengthening the assumption that higher education is crucial in the nation building process as propounded by the UNESCO document, Prof. K B Powar is of the view as suggested by Peter F. Drucker that "knowledge is the only meaningful resource today. The traditional 'factors of production' land (i.e. natural resources), labour, capital have not disappeared, but they have become secondary. They can be obtained, and obtained easily, provided there is knowledge. And knowledge in the new meaning is knowledge as utility, knowledge as the means to obtain social and economic results."

It is unfortunate that at a time when the autonomous colleges are aggrieved at the way funds are given to them, this proposal of the Central Government will destroy any enthusiasm for keeping together a structure that will offer a better delivery system in the field of education. Even at the risk of sounding very materialistic, one has to take congnizance of the necessity of good financial support, even in education, if it is to be meaningful to those who have to cope with the ever changing demands on their intelligence and knowledge.

As admitted by the Principals of Autonomous Collegs at the Workshop held in Madras during 7-8 April 1995, all the autonomous colleges face constraints in implementing the spirit of autonomy conferred upon them because of the restricting clauses in the use of allotted funds as well as the delay in the release of funds by the UGC (situation is now better). The indirect constraint imposed by the state government through the delay in fulfilling its commitment to the appointment of adequate number of teaching/non-teaching staff and worse still, the lethargy in filling up the vacancies of retired teaching staff which erodes the efficiency of the autonomous structure. The autonomous colleges have to abide by the rules of the government in the recruitment of teachers, thereby blocking the selection of a specialist, giving him financial incentives to teach a new area of study. Because of the work-load factor,which is yet to be decided by several state governments, weighing heavily with the allotment of funds by the government, many teachers are disinclined to take up innovative instruction strategies or even research projects. There is also the frustration resulting from the compulsion to use the funds as allocated and not in areas where most needed. Although it is edifying to note that the UGC wants a high standard in terms of qualifications, specialisation and experience, delay in filling up of posts on the basis of qualifications such as a Principal will slacken the progress of the institution, not to speak of the hardship to the learners who have to be satisfied with inadequate guidance. There is also the inability to offer new courses and degrees without the concurrence of the parent university. Of late some universities have begun to levy huge endowment fees on new courses of study in all colleges, indirectly crying halt to many well-established colleges from starting innovative programmes, as they cannot find the extra funds to pay for such courses. To augment the financial resources of the university, the affiliated colleges are taxed for being innovative while starting new courses. There is no provision to appoint part-time teachers in specialised courses.

The university administration through its apex bodies such as the Syndicate and the Senate is often not fully in tune with the spirit of the functioning of autonomous colleges. There is constant interference, imposing uniformity and dictating patterns of conformity. Administrative autonomy especially from the parent university still remaining a distant dream. This is worst experienced in matters pertaining to admission of students and especially in the increase of intake. Some universities have sanctioned autonomy only to UG courses, leaving P.G. and M. Phil. degrees. Much worse, the same college has autonomy for classes in day sections, while classes in the evening sections are non-autonomous.

Any casual observer will easily notice the incresse in paper-work involving maintenance of records with regard to continuous assessment, periodic evaluation, attendance, preparation of annual reports and others. Also the semester system with continuous assessment increases the workload of the staff. This additional quantum of work is to be noted by the State Government, while fixing workload pattern, and autonomous colleges need separate norms of workload. Teachers in autonomous colleges need recognition from the UGC and State Goverrnments when unique innovations in curriculum have been implemented. The meritorious students in these colleges are sore when their ranks are not considered for awards in the list of university ranks. Mobility of students from autonomous colleges for admission to PG courses in non-autonomous colleges often betrays discrimination by the latter. Credibility of the internal assessment is often questioned. *Added to this is the tale of woe from Autonomous Government Colleges, where teachers are constantly on transfer, thus affecting continuity.*

What emerges from an analysis of these experiences of the autonomous colleges is that the infrastructural requirements such as finance, staff, approval etc. are considered per se, rather independently in a highly bureaucratic manner without relating them to the objectives of autonomy which according to the UGC document "shall be a means to achieve higher standards and greater creativity in the future". The confusion has arisen because the UGC has been overcautious in not allowing any misunderstanding of autonomy as total freedom both financial and academic and so it has been careful to stipulate how the autonomous colleges will be held accountable to the UGC, the state government and the parent university. Such a control is necessary for the accreditation of an institution. But when this control, instead of being a benevolent, and enlightened kind of control turns out to be stifling mainly because of the controlling agencies' own lethargy, inefficiency and lack of vision, then the participants in the project are the losers. The loss is a serious one because of the mismatch between claims and implementation and this, in turn, may spread various types of pseudo concepts which will pass for sound educational achievements.

Since the major problems in the way of achieving quality and excellence arise out of the financial means available to the autonomous colleges, it will be approprite to consider some ways to ensure a timely flow of the required grant.

In the Report of the Dr. S. Muthukumaran, State-level Review Committee on Autonomous Colleges in Tamil Nadu, submitted in November 1991, the following suggestions have been made:

1. The UGC should continue to assist autonomous colleges.

2. There should be no delay in the sanction/release of funds.

3. The State government at least on a trial basis could sanction 'block grants' to autonomous colleges as on the lines of the State government's sanction of block grants to universities.

4. Alternatively, the State government could bear all the capital expenditure items of autonomous colleges, leaving the maintenance/salary expenditure to be borne by the concerned colleges, by allowing them to restructure fees payable by students. In fact, this will be in keeping with the spirit of NPE 1986.

5. Autonomous colleges should explore the possibilities of resource generation through consultancy services by the faculty members.

6. Surplus examination funds could be used for campus development, which is currently subject to Government audit.

7. Colleges should economise on expenditure.

Along with these, the following could also be considered:

a) The ceiling of Rs. 4 lakhs, Rs. 6 lakhs, and Rs. 7 lakhs per annum for different types of colleges could now be revised on the higher side, since these figures were appropriate to conditions a decade ago;

b) When funds are not needed for building, the college should be permitted to use it for giving remuneration to more additional/temporary staff.

c) Colleges should be permitted to appoint part-time teachers in specialised application oriented courses out of UGC grants.

d) The UGC and the State government should coordinate their norms and activities and not act in opposition to each other.

In the revised guidelines on autonomy, the UGC has outlined clauses, which were earlier found to be unacceptable to private college managements. One of the apprehensions of the universities in giving autonomy to colleges is that the universities are afraid of going out of business, once the supervisory activities and conduct of examination are taken away from them. Universities could be supervisory bodies for autonomous colleges in a more meaningful and constructive manner than they are at present. They will therefore be in a position to take care of the aspects which the Government or the UGC expects the governing bodies of autonomous colleges to do without, at the same time hampering the autonomy of private managements or of the Trusts.

For the effective functioning of autonomy, various academic and administrative bodies have been provided by the UGC. Autonomous colleges have not only constituted them following the UGC norms, but also have truly achieved in securing a participatory approach of management. The representatives to these bodies to be appointed by the UGC/the State government sometimes from the Universities are either delayed or lack the knowledge of the working of the autonomous system.

With regard to teacher identity in autonomous colleges the research report submitted by P. Palamottom (1992) has said that more than half the number are involved in efforts to improve their professional competence, such as involvement in major research projects, publications of research articles and books, participation in and conducting of refresher courses. In spite of the already existing heavy workload, involvement in research is credible. What is now demanded by teachers in these institutions is a clear and distinct preference of their major research projects in the UGC. Certain departments of autonomous colleges known for their outstanding research output and potential could be singled out to offer refresher courses, in collaboration with Academic Staff Colleges. In the past such proposals from select autonomous colleges have not been considered by State Councils of Higher Education.

Teachers of autonomous colleges are not averse to being evaluated by their colleagues, students and outside agencies. In some institutiions such an devaluation is in vogue while in others teachers voluntarily submit themselves to evaluation. Several autonomous colleges have opted for accreditation by NAAC. But the question is, after accreditation/autonomy, what? Where do we move from here? After twenty years of autonomy where does this experience and experiment land you in? Where does the march of autonomy lead to?

As a result of becoming autonomous, most colleges have evolved meaningful curriculum and better teaching methods. In the context of evolving an alternative agenda for higher education for the 21st century, autonomous colleges are being challenged to respond adequately to developments in communication and information technology. There is a need to re-engineer educational system using IT as a tool for assimilation, procuring and for providing value addition to all spheres of knowledge. There is a need therefore specially for autonomous colleges to be aware of the emerging pedagogic trends and strive to incorporate them in curriculum. The foremost concern now is to nurture and promote media attitude and media habit among teachers and students which would lead to media technology in instructional realm.

Autonomous colleges need to actively collaborate and co-operate among themselves. There is a need for a *Consortium of Autonomous Colleges*, which will serve as a forum to provide exchange of academic information among themselves and between universities. In this context, various measures especially several workshops conducted in the past few years by the Southern Region of the UGC, to bring together faculty from various autonomous colleges are to be commended.

Autonomous colleges had vowed to fulful a mission—a mission which will ultimately benefit the nation's growth, because of its investment in knowledge. Funding agencies should be able to appreciate the nature of the work involved in the autonomous colleges and facilitate their smooth and efficient functions. The autonomous colleges are not asking for concessions; they only demand their right to be served in a manner appropriate to demands of the task they have undertaken. A judicious and intelligent appraisal of the parameters within which these autonomous colleges have to operate will enable them to improve the human resources potential of our nation. Conferring of autonomy has been a right step in the field of higher education. As a coordinating organ of the Central Government, the UGC can create conditions by which the States Governements and Universities assist the progress of autonomous colleges and even their growth into deemed universities.

References:

1. Adisheshiah, Malcom, 1974, Objectives of Autonomous Colleges, *New Frontiers in Education*, Vol. IV, No.2, April-June.

2. Government of India, 1966, *Report of the Education Commission (1964-66): Education and National Developmant (Kothari Commission Report)*, Government of India, New Delhi.

3. ______,1986, *National Policy on Education, 1986*, Department of Education, Ministry of Human Resource Development, Government of India, New Delhi.

4. Government of Tamil Nadu, 1991, *Report of the State Level Review Committee on Autonomous Colleges in Tamil Nadu.*

5. Peter F. Drucker, 1974, *Management: Tasks, Responsibilities, Practices*, Harper & Row, New York.

6. ______, 1993, *Post Capitalist Society*, Butterworth Heinemann, New York.

7. Power, K.B., 1998, Government Support for Higher Education, *University News*, 36(24), June 15,1998. AIU, New Delhi.

8. Psacharapoulos, George, Tan, Jee, P. and Jimmenz, E., 1986, *Financing Education in Developing Countries: An Exploration of Policy Options, World Bank, Washington.*

9. University Grants Commission, 1993, *UGC Funding of Institutions of Higher Education (Punnaya Committee Report)*, UGC, New Delhi.

10.———,1997, *Report on the Recommendations of the Punnaya Committee relating to unit cost of Higher Education and other issues, (Pylee Committee Report)*, UGC, New Delhi.

11. Verghese, P. Palemattam, 1992, Emerging Style of Management in Higher Education, *University News.*

12.———, 1993, A Study of the Management of Autonomous Colleges with special focus on Innovation and Change, *New Frontiers in Education*, XXIII, No. 3, Jul-Sep. 358-367.

Chapter 11

Autonomous Colleges - A Royal Road to Civilization

*Prof. Dr. R.P.Choudhury

INDIA is a country where great teachers flourished and spread their knowledge to the students across the country. The bonds between teacher and students were strong and affectionate marked by an abiding concern from teacher and a disciplined application from the student. Today the need is to reclaim the past glory of teaching and revive the bonds of teacher-students relationship. Statistically speaking, there has been a quantum jump in the growth of schools and colleges and students at all levels. A tragic slump in the standard of teaching and learning can be noticed. Children from diverse background now come to schools, to colleges to seek instruction. This is a challenge to class teachers. The teacher should act as a facilitator and help bring out the best in the backward, average and gifted students.

Problems of Autonomous Colleges and Universities

Indian Universities have come to be known "Ivory Towers" due to a lack of relevance of their curriculum to societal problems. Rigidities in the Boards of the Studies do not allow redesigning of courses. The mismatch between higher education and employment is glaring.

The Universities have failed to perform even their minimum and basic tasks, such as making admissions, completing courses, conducting examination, declaring results, awarding degrees, payment of remuneration, etc. Examination system is in a mess. Complaints of short-supply of papers, printing errors, sealed envelopes containing no papers or wrong papers are reported on a wide scale. Far more serious are the reports of mass copying and leakages of question papers. As a consequence of easy granting of permission to start new universities, the academic system has been flooded with bogus degrees.

Principal, Khallikote Autonomous College, Berhampur (Orissa)

Remedial Measures for Higher Education

1. It is suggested that Autonomous colleges should take steps to introduce innovative and application-oriented programmes in every subject area.

2. Entrance examination should be conducted by autonomous colleges for students to its +3 course, PG, M.Phil. & Ph.D programmes.

3. Each autonomous college should organise more seminars and co-curricular activities and also field work programmes.

4. In every autonomous college curriculum development, improvement of syllabi and evaluation methods be undertaken frequently.

5. To improve student-teacher relationship, seminars, lectures, tutorials and group discussions be organised with student participation. Further, sincerity in implementing proctorial system is essential.

6. System of academic accountability has to be introduced.

7. Quarterly academic inspection has to be carried out at college level and university level.

8. Traditional mode of setting question papers should be dispensed with immediately.

9. Objective type of questions should be introduced in application-oriented and job-oriented papers.

10. There should be restructuring of syllabus at frequent intervals.

11. Restructuring of technical education, its framework and syllabus require a unique partnership of govt., industry and labour as well as social action organisations and universities. The success of this system will depend upon the effectiveness of the partnership

12. The autononmous colleges may introduce self-financing courses, which should be relevant to the area specially catering to the local needs, Financial self-reliance should be one of the important hallmarks of an autonomous institution.

13. Subjects like G.K., Current affairs, books by Swamy Vivekananda, *Discovery of India* by Jawaharlal Nehru, *My Experiments with Truth* by Mahatma Gandhi, the teachings of Bhagwan Sri Satya Sai and a study of the functioning of Sri Satya Sai University, *Prasantinilayam*, etc. will be a milestone in the progress of higher education in Indian style.

14. Finally, higher education should be modernised with the introduction of computer technology, without which the future Indian Educational System is bound to be bleak.

Examination and Evaluation

I. The question paper setter may be given valuation work also.

2. The Continuous Internal Assessment may be introduced by all the universities and autonomous colleges with uniform and equal weightage. While deciding the merit of a student his overall performance including attendance, home assignments, responses in classrooms be given due importance.

3. To avoid erratic valuation the valued scripts may be given to the students for scrutiny, wherever possible.

4. For central valuation experienced teachers working outside the university area may be invited. In case of external valuation, if an examiner fails to send the marksheet and valued scripts on or before the stipulated date, such examiner need not be given valuation work in future.

Feedback

The utility of syllabi should be monitored very closely. Improving the standards will help fulfilling expectations of the various sectors of the society. The success of feedback are :

* Comparison of syllabi offered by other autonomous colleges and universities will be available.

* Feedback from employers / Industrial and Technological institutions / Research and Development organisations could be sought.

* Organisation of seminars / symposia / workshops / interaction should be inter-departmental, inter-university, as far as it is possible be encouraged.

* Expert opinion in Boards of Study / Review committees on autonomy / inspection committee reports will be easily available

* Publication of Literatures / magazines could be made possible.

* The students self evaluation could be encouraged.

* Performance of candidates in competitive examinations, GATE, G-MAT may be monitored.

Total Quality Control for Human Resource Development

The problem of unemployment among the youth is directly linked with the problem of violence in the society. If the former is tackled with vision and foresight, the latter will get resolved to a significant degree almost automatically. The urgency is to prepare higher educational institutions to accept the need for change and to take necessary steps to facilitate changes for minimising the growth of unemployable degree-holders.

Let us hope that the planners, thinkers, intellectuals and various governments will tackle problems of unemployment and gear up the institutions of higher education in this new and most important direction with suitable changes in the courses of study and also in the mode of educational transactions. "Quality in Higher Education" and linking of it with "employment" (direct or indirect or self) are certainly the focus of attention in the present and also in the future.

Conclusion

The system needs an overall change, a change for the better, a change which is necessary if we want to regain our lost glory and become one of the most progressive countries of the world. It is inevitable that we adopt new approaches to rectify our past mistakes. Autonomous colleges should be revamped so that they can become centres of WORK, WORSHIP AND WISDOM.

———oooooooo———

RECOMMENDATIONS

After the inaugural session where the Chairperson, UGC, and several others from Pune University and the Centre had spoken the business session started with Dr. (Mrs.) Hamida Ahmed, Member UGC in the Chair.

Father Joseph Xavier of Loyola College, Chennai, Dr. S.D. Chand from Ewing Christian College, Allahabad spoke on examinations in their colleges. Fr. Xavier wanted the examination be phased out and replaced by a continuous internal assessment of 50 marks comprising assignments, project work, seminars etc. He advocated the setting up of a Grievance Committee to resolve problems being faced by students. Whereas revaluation be abolished the numer of times a student could take an examination be not limited. Question Banks be set up for being useful.

Dr. Chand wanted 75% attendance be made compulsory for taking an exam. With mid- term examination as a necessity multiple type of questions be preferred over the essay type. The ratio between the internal and external be fixed at 50% each. Sharing his own experience as Principal of the College he mooted one suggestion of forming a consortium of autonomous colleges in each region which could fix standards, award degrees etc. One should plan for credit based system. He informed the Conference that students favoured semester system.

CHAPTER 12
STUDENTS' FEEDBACK MECHANISM AND QUALITY ASSURANCE

* DR. L. Jayalakshmi

1:1 Introduction

1:2 Paradigm shift in the Perspective of Higher Education

1:3 Reasons for the Paradigm Shift

1:4 Students Feedback Strategy

1:5 Students Feedback in other Countries and in India

1:6 Reasons for the non-acceptance/non-adoption of Students Feedback

2:1 Students Feedback Mechanism in an Autonomous College

2:2 Summary account of the Students Feedback

2:3 Follow up of the Students Feedback Conclusion

1:1 Introduction

India has one of the largest systems of higher education in the world, with her gigantic network of 234 Universities, 11,000 colleges, 3 lakh teachers and 60 lakh students. So to say, the system of higher education in India is one of the biggest man-making enterprises in the world.

In terms of quantity, India's progress in Higher Education is rich but qualitatively it is poor. Mere numbers cannot be mistaken as indicators of progress. It is only a "Quantitative Junk" as stated by Alexander (1995)[1].

1:2 Paradigm shift in the perspective of Higher Education

In the context of Globalization, Privatization and Liberalization the educational scenario is getting through a period of transition from quantitative expansion to qualitative improvement.

Principal, Sri G. V. G. Visalakshi College for Women (Autonomous), (Affiliated to Bharathiar University) Udamalpet - 642 128 Coimbatore Dt., Tamil Nadu.

This process of transition warrants a paradigm shift in the perspective of education. The erstwhile concept of deeming education a man-making process, with its stress on the renaissance spirit of enquiry and humanism, has been dealt a death blow and in its place has emerged a New Education Pattern operating on the principle of 'consumerism' with emphasis on 'consumer satisfaction', 'cost effectiveness' and 'teacher accountability' (1998)[2]. This new wave must be taken in its stride without much lament. Rostogi is absolutely justified in using the jargon of consumerism.

1:3 The reasons for the paradigm shift in the perspective of education

- the investment in education in terms of physical and human resources has grown tremendously over the last five decades. Everyone now wants education as part of social system to be accountable for resources.

- educational institutions have an obligation to the society because they are provided with the funds and resources by the society. Therefore, the society has the right to know and judge their performance.

- education today is no longer confined to the development of intellectual powers or the knowledge of the abstract type, but to the development and promotion of skills and know how for the industrial productivity, for the production of goods and service for the global markets.

- education as an organic entity, changes, grows with the time, responds to the needs of the society and adopts itself to the environment. It was mostly an ornament in the agricultural civilization, a tool in economic development in the industrial era. But today (in the 21st century) education has become an all pervasive resource, a resource that can find substitutes for other resources but has no substitute for itself says V.C. Kulandaiswami,(1998)[3].

Therefore more than ever, now there is the dire need to tone up the quality of education on an emergency footing. To quote the UGC 'development of higher education in India faces the challenge of quantity versus quality and a strategy has to be evolved to arrive at an acceptable balance between the two (1997)[4].

1:4 Students' Feedback Strategy to tone up Quality and Establish Quality Assurance

- Students feedback has been one of the feedback mechanisms in the process of toning up quality and establishing quality assurance.

- The structure of any institution of higher learning is mainly supported by THREE CONSTITUENTS viz. Teachers, Students and Administrative Staff. Education system is a complex system as it involves human beings as input to and output from the system. Students are the input and the customers too. Both in terms of numbers and capability university students represent a single most potent force in society and exercise a powerful influence in the contemporary world.

- The origin of students' evaluation of teaching can be traced back to the time of Socrates in the West and Panini in the East. Such informations were gathered informally and unsystematically. Western and developed countries have the 100 year long and rich tradition of adopting the systematic Teacher Evaluation by Students (1996)[5].

1:5 Students' Feedback in other countries and India

In many developed countries students' evaluation of teachers is a regular feature. Students feedback are taken into account at the time of appointments and promotion of teachers.

In Australia, the National Union of Students in 1990 made the main demand "we want good teaching". The reason was that most teachers there had become interested in research on which depended their promotions and as such, they were neglecting teaching.

The students even insisted that teachers should always be appointed on contract and students should be consulted at the time of renewal of these contracts. All candidates for fresh appointments have to give seminars in which the students have a right to be present and to give their opinion about the teaching abilities of the candidates and their opinion have to be taken into account at the time of appointments (1997)[6].

In our country the University Grants Commission has been insisting on the need to have the Students' Feedback for assessing the efficiency of teachers. The UGC has conducted a few workshops and came out with the suggestion that the process of assessment of students should be continuous and the students in turn may also anonymously conduct evaluation of the teachers with a view to assessing the efficiency of teachers in the teaching process. Such a feedback mechanism is necessary to identify the weaknesses and deficiencies in instruction, so that continuous improvement could be effected (1991)[7].

The Gnanam Committee Report acknowledges that the Society is entitled to demand that the members of the academic community individually and collectively be made accountable in concrete, visible terms (1990)[8].

Amrik Singh advocates that "efforts should be made to introduce some system of students' feedback. While integrating the reactions of students the opinions of academically more mature and motivated students receive a higher weightage" (1995)[9].

The recently concluded UNESCO World Conference on Higher Education declares that full academic freedom and autonomy should be given for Higher Education which should at the same time be accountable to society (1998)[10].

In our country, students feedback mechanism has been in operation in the IITs for a long time (The IIT governing system, appointment method, promotion rules and admission norms are in no way comparable to the university and college systems in our country).

St. Xaviers College and Sophia College both Mission controlled colleges located in Bombay have been following this for about two decades.

1:6 Reasons for the non-acceptance non adoptation of the Students Feedback in the Arts & Science Colleges of our country

Presently, there is no formal method of assessing the work of a teacher except for the degree/diploma/certificate he posseses. Generally teacher evaluation through the students is not administratively required in the Indian educational systems.

A review of literature on students Evaluation of Teacher reveals that this area has been thoroughly investigated only by the researches abroad.

But in India, only after the Mehrotra's and Rostogi Commission Reports many theoretical articles for and against SET have been published in many journals and magazines. These have brought this issue as a controversial one

As Vadhera (1998)[11] remarks "the startling fact is that not even a single empirical study has been conducted on Students Feedback of Teachers . So to say, the research area of teacher evaluation by students is relatively a virgin area in India".

Students Feedback or Students Evaluation of Teacher (SET) has been opposed on the following grounds.

- students cannot make a consistent judgement about the teachers and their teaching due to immaturity.

- they would be influenced by extraneous factors like caste, religion, etc.

- they could be exploited by vested interests to give opinion in their favour.

- would lead to a trade off between teachers and students.

- teachers might do anything and everything possible on their part to get better things from the students.

- might be misused by the administrator to harass and humiliate teachers.

In the light of the absence of any empirical research studies in the India context, it may not be possible to confirm the above narrated apprehensions of teachers about the students, feedback.

But research studies in the developed countries spanning over six decades in relation to the apprehensions of teachers about students feedback or students evaluation did not support the concerns of the teachers (1996)[12].

In general, the research studies conclude that students ratings tend to be statistically reliable, valid and relatively free from bias, probably more than any other data used for faculty evaluation (1996)[13].

It is strange that we can trust illiterate voters to give their opinion about political candidates, but cannot trust the educated students to give their opinion about their teachers and this is in spite of the fact that there has been almost no case where students have been asked to give their opinion and the students have given only based opinion. We can trust our teachers to examine students in an unbased manner but we cannot trust our students to assess their teachers. Therefore, the mistrust on the part of teachers about the students ability to evaluate teachers in the classroom setting is an unfortunate one.

In the present scenario of higher education becoming global in its reach toning up quality through students feedback has become inevitable. The theoretical and empirical and the existing environment demonstrate that a considerable amount of useful information can be obtained from students feedback towards quality build up and quality assurance in Higher Education.

Students elsewhere have brought about revolutions and changed governments. Cannot our students try to get good education and good teaching?

That is why, Amrik Singh (1995) advocates that "a well organised and scientific system of academic audit (SET) would have to be given top priority even if it is going to give some marginal improvements in higher education." Considering the potency and importance of students' feedback as a quality toning method, the National Assessment and Accreditation Council has identified student feedback as one among the 10 parameters for accrediting public and private institutions of higher learning (1997)[14] From the above analysis it is to be accepted that the use of students feedback can be one of the effective tools for the total quality management of institutions of higher education.

2:1 Students Feedback Mechanism as it is in Vogue in an Autonomous College (Sri G.V.G. Visalakshi College for Women, Udamalpet)

Quality is a process of continuous improvement and the key to quality improvement should *focus on the process and not on the product.*

Concern for quality and relevance of education is highlighted in educational policies nationally and globally. Students and administrators should monitor the quality of teaching whereas teachers and parents the quality of learning.

Students are the partners and prime beneficiaries of Higher Education, their evaluation/assessment of the academic packages in terms of the syllabi, teaching and evaluation would go a long way in identifying the weaknesses and deficiencies, so that continuous improvements could be effected.

Autonomous Colleges have a very conducive environment with the grassroot level participation of the teachers both in the academic working of Autonomy and the governance of Autonomy. Students are also given representation in the Boards of Studies & Academic Council of the college. To a large extent, there is the participatory management of Autonomous Colleges by the Principals, Teachers and Students.

Further, Autonomy is a move from a closed system to an open ended, expandable and flexible system, from prescription to creation and from the static curriculum to a dynamic curriculum.

Against this backdrop, the Autonomous Colleges as the pace setters in Higher Education through relevance and quality of the courses, are better placed to adopt the Students' Feedback strategy.

Academic standards/quality can be improved by breaking the academic process into a number of sub-processes and each one of them is attended to, enriched and streamlined (Amrik Singh 1995)[15].

Accordingly the college had obtained the feedback of the students regarding

1. Governance of Autonomy
2. Syllabuses
3. Teaching
4. Evaluation (Internal and External)

Governance of Autonomy — particularly the rules and regulations framed by the college to implement the Autonomous Scheme. The college has brought out a booklet on the same. At the time of admissions, each student was given a copy of this and asked to study before coming to the college.

To make them have a good awareness of the rules and regulations, and an orientation programme on the various aspects of Autonomy was organised by the senior students. Ten senior students preferably from the third year were selected to talk about the various aspect of Autonomy and that was followed by an interaction session with the freshers.

The interaction was very encouraging and their doubts were all cleared. This way, we make sure that the students are made aware of and well conversant with the Autonomous curriculum and the other aspects· With this orientation, the college would start functioning in terms of curricular, co-curricular and extra-curricular activities.

At the end of each semester, the curriculum devlopment cell and the evaluation committee would get the feedback of the students on

1. Syllabuses— course contents
2. Teaching
3. Evaluation (Internal arld External)

2:2 Summary account ofthe Students' Feedback

It would be very exhaustive to present the outcomes of students evaluation. However, a capsule account of the same is given below :

i. Highlights

ii. Inadequacies

iii. Suggestions

i. Highlights

- Syllabi are good with the thrust on modern contents and application orientatioin.

- appreciated the importance given to co and extra curricullar activilies.
-commended the timely conduct of examinations and prompt publication of results.

- welcome the inclusion of Self Study modules in each paper, to promote auto learning and to develop reference skills and reading habits.

- internal assessment helps them to be regular in their learning.

- weightage for attendance motivates them to be prompt in attending the classes.

ii. Inadequacies

- Overlaping of portions in some papers like Statistics, Modern algebra and Mathematical Physics.

- Medical Instrumentation papers are heavy and vast.

- in the place of Chemistry, Zoology students want Bio-chemistry as allied subject.

- lack of practicals for the paper "Computer Applications in Business".
- shortage of reference books for some subjects like Environmental Economics, Computer Applications in Business, Laboratory Techniques etc, Bio-chemistry, Environmental Science etc.

iii. Suggestions

- Allotment of more library hours to take care of self study portions and to prepare for competitive examinations.

- increased use of A.V. room to facilitate effective learning.

- inclusion of a compulsory paper on computer learning as a need-based paper for all the students.

- facilities to learn additional languages like Hindi, German, French

- prescription of inspiring books for study under Part I.

- the calender of the academic events should be given well in advance to know the run of events from teaching till the publication of results and issue of mark sheets.

- interested sludents must be permitted to participate in more than our co-curricular activity.

- the awarding of 5 marks for 100% attendance should be changed to 90%.

2:3 Follow up of the Students' Feedback

The feedback was intimated to the faculty and the Boards of Studies. To a large extent, these suggestions were incorporated in the curriculum as pointed out below :

- Computer learning is incorporated in the syllabi for all I year students stretching over two semesters.

- A certificate course and a Diploma course in computer learning are started to facilitate the Second and Third year students to accquire computer literacy.

- Under Part I a paper 'History of Tamil Literature' is kept with the IAS syllabus to motivate them to take up competitive examinations.

- Enriching the library in terms of books found inadequate in certain areas is an ongoing activity.

- Two A.V. rooms well equipped with a colour TV, a Deck, OHP, a slide projector and audio video cassettes have been set up to have more of audio video learning.

- Facility to learn Hindi outside the class time has been created within the campus. The college is the recognized centre for conducting the examination. 'Diploma in Hindi' and Certificate in Hindi, conducted by the Department of Correspondence Course, Central Hindi Directorate. Ministry of Human Resource Development, New Delhi and Dhakshina Bharath Hindi Prachar Sabha- Chennai and Trichi.

- Distributed the calendar of academic events to all the students in the beginning of the academic year.

- reduced the percentage of attendance from 100 to 97 to earn the full marks (5 marks).

- have kept inspiring books for study under Part-1

I dare	— by Kiran Bedi
Ennangal	— by M.S.Udayamoorthi
I.A.S. Thervum Anugumuraiyum	— by V. Iraianbu I,A,S

Students evaluation of teachers was in terms of the proper spread and coverage of the portion, punctuality in coming to the class, articulating abilities, promptness in the return of the test papers, assignments, use of teaching aids etc.

A structured proforma was given to the students to evaluate the teacher and they were clearly oriented about the purpose of evaluation.

The filled-in forms were consolidated and the areas of deficiencies were informed to the teachers concerned with a reformative approach.

We took the following precautions while getting the feedback.

Not to use this as an administrative tool for harassing the teachers or giving an upperhand for the students to humiliate the teachers. We made it very clear to both the teachers and the taught that it is only a diagnostic exercise to improve the teaching-learning.

Students were asked to be anonymous in giving their views/ opinion.

Conclusion

With the feedback recieved on Syllabi, Teaching and Evaluation as an Autonomous College, we could enrich the syllabi with the addition of the required and relevant inputs, strengthen it by deleting irrelevant and overlapping portions and add more dynamism and practical orientation through A.V. teaching, Practicals, Project work, and Field visits.

Reference:

1. Dr. P.C. Alexander *"Convocation Address" Scientific Temper, University News,* August 1995 Pg. 16.

2. Dr. P. Thailambal *"Students Assessment of Teachers", University News,* March 2, 1998 Pg.1.

3. Mr. V.C. Kulandaisamy, *University News,* April 20, 1998 Pg.5.

4. University Grants Commission - *Report of the year 1995-96 presented to the Govt. of India* Pg.3.

5. Chandra Kant Bhogayata *"Students Evaluation of University Teaching",* University News, October 7, 1996 Pg.12.

6. J.N. Kapur *"Students Attitude to Higher Education" University News,* September 15, 1997 Pg.13.

7. Srinivasa Narayanaswamy *"Evaluation of Teachers by Students", University News,* September5, 1991 Pg.7.

8. A. Gnanam *"Accountability in Higher Education",* AIU, New Delhi, 1995.

9. Amrik Singh *"The Trap Called Teaching - Reflections on Teaching and Teachers,* Konark Publishers Pvt. Ltd., New Delhi, 1995, Price 225, Pg.229.

10. A Landmark Conference on Education, Editorial Column"*The Hindu'* 21-10-98.

11. Ram Pal Vadhera *"Students Evaluation of Teachers- An Opinion Survey of Teachers",* University News, July 27, 1998 Pg.7.

12. Chandra Kanth Bhogayata *"Students Evaluation of University Teaching",* University News, October 7,1996 Pg.14.

13. *Ibid* Pg.15.

14. *'NAAC's "Assesment and Accreditation Process"* 1998 Pg.6.

15. Amrik Singh *"The Trap Called Teaching",* 1995 Pg.74.

Recommendations on Students Feedback

Dr. (Mrs.) Sudha Rao, Senior Fellow from NIEPA presented her study after Mrs. Jayalakshmi, on 'Students Feedback Mechanism'. Her study revealed that chalk and talk method was still very popular. Students showed a positive preference for the semester system and internal evaluation. In the autonomous colleges 90% teachers were found better prepared for classes and the relationship between students and teachers was markedly better than elsewhere. The other positive points included job-oriented courses, market surveys and collection of student requirements etc.

However, transfer of teachers was a point of major concern for these colleges and called for remedial correction.

Dr. (Mrs.) Jayalakshmi, Principal, V.G. Visalakshi College for Women, T. N. talked of student's feedback first. She reported that for quality improvement this mechanism was a major contributory factor. Participative management was found a highly satisfying experience. Rules were made through consensus and the students liked both the content of curriculum and other activities while they welcomed internal assessment. Students wanted more library hours, audio-visual room, and diplomas in areas where none exist. They also wanted to evaluate their teachers, though only anonymously.

After the Chairperson, Miss Desai had summed up the presentations and briefly remarked that autonomous colleges were on the whole succeeding, the group made the following recommendations.

The group considered favourably the expansion of autonomy in colleges and recommnended the following:

A) Promoting autonomy by way of creating awareness and meaningful understanding of autonomy and its advantages. UGC may take up some promotional activity involving the existing autonomous colleges.

B) Seminars and other academic enrichment programmes arranged for Faculty of Autonomous Colleges may be extended to other teachers in that area so that they would also be motivated and updated.

C) A greater co-ordinatioin between autonomous colleges in different regions may be encouraged through a system of consortium for Autonomous Colleges in that region. The consortium could consider sharing of resources both in terms of infrastructural facilities and academic expertise. The consortium could think of offering joint academic programmes through collaborative efforts. A self monitoring and evalulation process to upgrade the system could also be evolved by the consortium.

It was brought to the notice of the group that some of the States have unified undergraduate syllabi which have to be implemented even in Autonomous Colleges. Hence the committee recommends that the UGC take appropriate measures so that these Autonomous Colleges are empowered to design their own undergraduate curriculum following the recommended norms and guidelines set by UGC.

In the state of MP where the number of Government colleges are about 40 and where almost all autonomous colleges are government colleges, a different system or pattern of autonomy exists. It is recommended that in the even set up, it should be feasible to seek option of teachers regarding their being in an autonomous set up. Similarly, appropriate selection procedures (entrance tests) may be adapted, giving certain degree of option to students as well. In this process, we'll be able to attract teachers who are motivated and convinced about Autonomy. It is also recommended that non-collegiate (private) students should be educated through Open University or Distance Education Programmes.

D) With the advancement of IT, the autonomous colleges may be provided with internet facility enabling access to educational resources, promoting research and academic co-operation between Autonomous Colleges.

Universities may adopt the following format :

e.g. B.A. Degree in Cooperation with Advertisement and Sales Promotion with vocational Subject.

i) The Director, Higher Education should insist on the adoption of student mechanism methods and maintain records properly.

ii) All this may be made mandatory.

iii) The UGC should provide some kind of orientation to both Principals and teachers of Autonomous Colleges. Some designated Academic Staff Colleges may be assigned this job specifically.

iv) For appreciating the problems faced by autonomous colleges UGC sponsored empirical research may be undertaken.

v) Active Parent-Teacher Associations.

vi) Feedback from the examinations about the contents of the courses and the quality of the performance of students.

vii) Organisation of Sammelans where students express their opinions freely.

viii) Regular meetings of Principals with Student Councils on day to day administration.

ix) Transparency in examination by returning the answerbooks to students.

x) Teachers' evaluation proforma was generally prepared with the help of outside experts/Planning and Evaluation Committee/Teachers themselves.

Following recommendations were made:

1. The colleges may adopt any/combined tools for the purpose of bringing about changes in a positive manner.

2. Colleges should explain the purpose of adopting feedback mechanisms as tools for quality enrichment.

3. The universities may be persuaded to spurn discriminatory behaviour towards autonomous colleges.

4. The certificates awarded by the college be also made acceptable.

CHAPTER 13

AUTONOMY AND STUDENTS' CONCERN

K. Sudha Rao*

Autonomy to the colleges has been one such programme of the education sector which has attracted attention of almost all those who are directly or indirectly linked with higher education system. Parents, teachers, students, polilticians and even common man has concern for the scheme. But mostly the reactions are not based on any authentic data. This presentation is aimed at providing data based information collected from those who are experiencing autonomy since its implementation in their respective colleges. The author has made efforts to collect data from different sets of sample, analysed them and placed under different headings for easy understanding of the readers.

Policies and programmes are generally targeted at improving the existing system and its functioning. The real effectiveness of such policies and programmes can be ascertained only by analysing the data collected from those who are either experienced or experiencing the programme, in other words, the ultimate beneficiary groups. Students being the beneficiaries of the Autonomous Scheme, the present study's emphasis is to collect data from the students alongwith others on the issue of autonomous scheme and its implementation in respective colleges. Questionnaire developed for the said purpose of eliciting the responses was administered to a representative sample group of 1021 students from sample colleges. Details of sample include students from colleges of different states (1) viz, Tamil Nadu, Andhra Pradesh and Rajasthan; (2) management**, (3) university***, (4) rural and urban (5) exclusively women, men and co-educational (6) with different religious affiliations such as Christian, Muslim, Hindu and general, (7) autonomous and non-autonomous colleges, and (8) colleges having different categories of students. The responses were analysed in aggregate and classified into different categories and are provided in the Tables I to IX. As the number

* Senior Fellow, NIEPA.

** Viz. Private and Government.

*** Andhra, Nagarjuna, Osmania, Bharatidasan, Bharathiar, Madras, Ajmer and Manonmaniam Sunderanariyar Universities.

selected from within the categories are not proportionate, the percentage calculated are in aggregate and the real difference can be ascertained in comparison with respective frequencies provided in each table and the concerned breakup of group. The responses of students from 19 autonomous colleges (ACs) and three non-autonomous colleges (NACs) of similar status have been included in the present study.

Students' Awareness about Autonomous Scheme

Though the scheme was initiated in late 1970s, it did not receive wider recognition. The major reason attributed to the situation is the lack of proper awareness among the teachers, students and even administrators. In order to assess the extent of awareness about the scheme, its successful implementation and its effect among the students, questions were directed towards this end. The findings reveal that 70% students were found familiar with the scheme, but it is equally necessary to note that 30% of the sampled students were found unaware of the scheme. It suggests that the awareness among the students is incomplete even amongst those studying in autonomous colleges.

The analysis, further reveals that the awareness among the students of the private colleges is rather higher in comparison the students from the government colleges. Similarly awareness among students of Ajmer University is comparatively lower than that of the other two states viz. Tamil Nadu and Andhra Pradesh. Rajasthan was amongst the very few states where autonomous scheme is implemented in only government colleges and the finding is revealing in terms of the differences between private and government autonomous colleges.

Impact on Students (Table I)

To the query on impact of the scheme on the quality aspects, such as concentration on study, discipline, creating enthusiasm in students etc., the responses are encouraging. It is learnt that ACs lay greater emphasis on study (83.4%), make students disciplined (77.0%), and breed enthusiasm in learning (72.8%).

The general apprehension that the system promotes favouritism by the teachers is there upto 66.1%. It is rooted in the fear amongst the students as the evaluation of answer sheets in the ACs is done by the teachers of the college, whereas in the affiliating system this responsibility rests with the university.

The state wise and university analysis of the impact of AC reveals that the pattern remains similar to that of the total sample. A majority of the students perceive that the scheme is beneficial to them in building their academic careers.

TABLE I
STUDENTS RESPONSE TOWARDS AUTONOMOUS SCHEME AND ITS IMPACT

(In Percentages)

	Student Awareness	Provides for choice in combination of courses	Promotes Emphasis on Study	Promotes discipline	Breeds Enthusiasm	Promotes Favoratism	Job oriented courses
Total (1021)	**70.0**	**80.2**	**83.4**	**77.8**	**72.8**	**66.1**	**55.4**
Managementwise							
Private (782)	56.6	64.4	64.4	63.2	58.2	54.5	46.2
Government (239)	13.4	15.8	15.8	13.8	14.6	11.6	9.2
Nature of College							
Men (96)	8.4	7.8	7.7	7.5	7.3	6.1	6.1
Women (222)	16.5	19.8	20.1	20.2	17.1	15.8	12.5
Co-Educational	45.2	52.5	55.5	49.4	48.1	44.1	36.7
Autonomous Status							
Autonomous (895)	61.7	70.6	73.1	67.7	64.0	57.5	49.2
Non Autonomous (126)	8.4	9.5	10.4	9+4	8.8	8.6	6.3
Statewise							
Andhra Pradesh (317)	19.6	24.1	24.5	22.5	21.3	18.3	13.6
Tamil Nadu (574)	45.6	49.6	52.7	49.5	45.6	43.0	39.2
Rajasthan,(130)	4.8	6.5	6.2	5.0	5.8	4.8	2.6
Universitywise							
Andhra (53)	3.2	4.1	4.5	4.4	3.4	3.0	1.9
Nagaruna (50)	5.1	4.7	4.8	4.8	4.5	4.2	3.5
Osmania (175)	11.3	15.3	15.3	13.3	13.4	11.1	8.2
Bharathidasan (141)	10.7	11.5	12.3	11.9	10.6	9.5	9.8
Bharathiar (111)	8.0	9.5	9.6	8.9	8.3	7.9	7.7 1
Madras (224)	18.6	17.5	19.2	17.6	17.7	16.7	13.4
Madurai Kamaraj (37)	2.8	2.5	3.2	2.7	2.9	2.1	2.2
Ajmer (130)	1 4.8	6.5	6.2	5.0	5.8	4.8	2.6
S.Manomania M (91)	5.5	8.4	8.4	8.4	6.1	6.8	6.1

Teaching Methods (Table II)

The scheme has been successful not only in providing greater freedom to the colleges in redesigning the courses but also in encouraging colleges to new methods of teaching as well. ACs have been trying different methods in addition to conventional methods of teaching, yet it is equally important to note that the conventional method of teaching persists in the classrooms. The "Chalk and Talk" method appears to be a powerful method behind which the human operates with both teacher and the taught which of course is responsible for its continuance.

The figures reveal that non-conventional methods of teaching like group discussions (25.3%), Seminars (41.5%), Project methods (23.9%), Question and Answer method (27.8%) and Lecture cum discussion method (39.7%) are also in vogue in addition to the conventional method of lecturing (74.7%). It is obvious from the data that teachers' priority is for conventional method and other methods though used are occasional. The project methods seems to be the least praticed method in almost all categories of colleges.

TABLE II
TEACHING METHODS AND ITS EFFECTIVENESS AS PERCEIVED BY STUDENTS

(In Percentages)

	Method						Effectiveness		
	Lecture method	Group Discussion	Seminars	Project Method	Question answer	Lecture Cum Discussions	Transmit of ideas	Behavioural-changes	Develop ment Skills
Total	**74.7**	**25.3**	**41.5**	**23.9**	**27.8**	**39.7**	**74.4**	**72.4**	**69.2**
Managementwise									
Private (782)	59.2	21.6	35.1	21.0	22.4	31.4	59.2	61.2	55.6
Govt. (239)	15.5	3.7	6.4	2.9	5.4	8.3	15.2	13.2	13.6
Nature of College									
Men (96)	7.2	1.6	1.8	1.0	3.0	2.9	7.4	7.0	6.7
Women (222)	17.0	8.2	10.4	1.2	8.0	11.2	18.1	17.3	17.5
Co-Educational (703)	50.5	15.5	29.3	15.7	16.8	25.6	48.9	48.1	45.0
Autonomous Status									
Autonomous College (895)	65.4	22.7	36.7	22.4	24.9	36.0	66.0	63.2	60.6
Non-Autonomous (126)	9.5	2.5	4.8	1.5	2.8	3.6	8.5	9.3	8.5
Statewise									
Andhra Pradesh (317)	20. 1	5.1	3.9	.6	6.7	11.3	20.7	21.0	18.8
Tamil Nadu (574)	46.2	18.5	34.2	21.3	18.7	24.5	46.6	45.8	45.3
Rajasthan(130)	8.4	1.5	3.4	1.0	2.4	3.9	7.1	5.6	5.1
Universitywise									
Andhra(53)	3.4	.7	1.0	.1	.7	.9	3.2	3.8	2.8
Nagarjuna(59)	4.7	.3	.6	.1	1.9	1.5	4.9	4.8	4.2
Osmania(175)	12.0	4.1	2.3	.4	4.1	8.9	12.6	12.4	11.8
Bharathidasan (141)	11.0	3.9	8.4	4.0	4.6	5.9	9.9	9.5	10.0
Bharathiar (111)	8.0	3.4	5.5	4.4	3.9	5.0	9.2	8.7	8.0
Madras (224)	17.5	5.6	12.2	8.7	6.0	8.6	18.4	18.2	17.9
M.Kamaraj(37)	2.4	1.2	2.0	.6	1.0	1.5	2.3	2.5	2.4
Ajmer (130)	8.4	1.5	3.4	1.0	2.4	3.9	7.1	15.6	5.1
S. Manomaniam (91)	7.3	4.6	6.1	4.6	3.2	3.5	6.8	6.9	7.0

Usage of Teaching Aids (Table III)

The students response reveal as under:

—	use of Blackboard	86.3%
—	use of Maps	45.8%
—	use of Pictures	38.1%
—	use of Models	38.2%
—	use of Films	35.7%
—	use of Computer	37.6%

The above response is to be viewed in the context of existing curriculum which is less practical, yet students are satisfied with whatever the present practice is in ACs and feel that teaching method is effective in transmitting the knowledge and skill required to the students.

Government Autonomous College seem to display a totally different picture. Not only in minimal change after getting autonomy but also in all other aspects of college such as restructuring, teaching methods, use of teaching aids etc.

Examination Reforms

All ACs are conducting their own examination. Some have introduced semester system while other are continuing with the annual pattern. Tamil Nadu and Andhra Pradesh Colleges set their own question papers, whereas in Rajasthan, Ajmer University sets the question paper for the use of Autonomous Colleges as well and the college only conducts the examination. As they have not introduced either semester system or continous evaluation, the gap between teacher and students continued to be the same in ACs as in the affiliated colleges in Rajasthan. More than 50 per cent (56.9%) of the students are satisfied with this type of examination system as well. ACs have generally fixed calendar of working days examination schedule. Further, most of the colleges (except Rajasthan) have implemented the semester system. Majority of students feel that the reforms in examination introduced in ACs have been successful in promoting creating abilities (66.7%), communication skills (54.1%), applicability of knowledge gained (62.3%) and subject understanding (59.2%).

TABLE III
USAGE OF TEACHING AIDS AS PERCEIVED BY STUDENTS

(In Percentages)

	Black Board	Maps	Pic-tures	Models	Film/ T.V.	Comp-puter
Total (1021)	**86.3**	**45.8**	**38.1**	**38.2**	**35.7**	**37.6**
Managementwise						
Private (782)	67.9	35.6	30.3	30.6	31.6	35.8
Government (239)	18.4	10.2	7.8	7.4	4.1	1.8
Nature of College						
Men (96)	7.6	3.4	3.3	2.4	3.2	2.4
Women (222)	17.9	8.1	8.1	9.1	6.9	8.9
Co-educational (703)	60.8	34.3	26.7	26.7	25.6	26.3
Autonomous Status						
Autonomous(895)	174.6	40.0	33.0	34.3	30.1	32.9
Non-Autonomous (126)	11.4	5.7	5.1	3.8	5.7	4.8
Statewise						
Andhra Pradesh (317)	26.9	15.2	9.9	11.2	8.6	13.3
Tamil Nadu (574)	47.9	23.9	235	22.6	23.3	23.6
Rajasthan (130)	11.3	6.7	4.7	4.4	2.8	.7
Andhra (53)	4.7	2.8	1.8	2.4	2.1	2.7
Nagarjuna (59)	5.8	2.4	2.5	2.0	2.6	2.2
Osmania (175)	16.4	10.0	5.6	6.8	3.9	8.4
Bharadhidasan (141)	11.5	5.3	5.7	5.3	7.6	7.1
Bharathiar (111)	9.6	3.3	4.3	4.7	4.8	5.3
Madras (224)	15.9	8.6	7.7	6.6	6.7	5.4
Madurai Kamaraj(37)	3.2	1.5	1.2	1.6	1.4	1.4
Ajmer (130)	11.3	6.7	4.7	4.4	2.8	.7
S. Manomaniam (91)	7.7	5.2	4.6	4.4	3.8	4.4

The inherent drawback of the examination system in the affiliating patter is that the students are tested mainly at the terminal point i.e. after completing one year of study.

TABLE IV
SATISFACTION OF STUDENTS WITH REGARD TO INFRASTRUCTURAL FACILITIES

(In Percentages)

	Good Library	Good Laboratory	Good Hostel
Total (1021)			
Management Wise			
Private (782)	43.7	42.0	42.1
Government (239)	14.7	13.3	11.8
Nature of College			
Men (96)	6.6	6.0	6.9
Women (222)	14.0	13.6	13.9
Co-educational(703)	37.8	35.7	33.1
Autonomous Status			
Autonomous (895)	52.3	50.3	49.7
Non-Autonomous (126)	6.1	4.9	4.2
Statewise			
Andhra Pradesh (317)	14.9	13.3	11.7
Tamil Nadu (574)	36.7	35.0	37.1
Rajasthan (1 30)	6.8	7.0	5.1
Universitywise			
Andhra (53)	1.6	2.4	2.4
Nagarjuna (59)	4.1	3.0	3.8
Osmania (175)	9.2	7.9	5.5
Bharathidasan (141)	8.6	10.0	10.6
Bharathiar (111)	6.4	5.8	6.9
Madras (224)	12.8	10.3	9.1
Madurai Kamaraj (37)	2.5	2.3	2.8
Ajmer (130)	6.8	7.0	5.1
S. Manomaniam (91)	6.4	6.6	7.7

This makes the students less serious in their studies till the end of the year. ACs. having got the freedom to reform the examination system. The colleges have successfully planned and introduced Continous Internal Assessment System (CIA). CIA takes into consideration the overall academic performance in and outside the classroom. The general apprehension is that the introduction of CIA may pollute the atmosphere of the college by sowing the seeds of favouritism and colleges may use this as a whip against students. On the contrary, University administrators' apprehension is that the colleges might boost the marks of their own students. No doubt the data supports CIA as successful in producing positive such as regular study (72.2%), make examination interesting and easy, reduces tension and anxiety, (74%) and helps to score marks (23.4%) are evidences to this.

Majority of ACs follow double evaluation system (Internal and External) of the answer scripts and the discrepancies are settled through generally accepted norms. This limits the chances of boosting of marks.

Insfrastructure Facilities (Table IV)

Autonomous Colleges are entitled to special financial assistance from the UGC, which provides minimum grant of Rs. 4 lakhs annually and each college enjoys freedom to use this in developing its infrastructure facilities. Students are satisfied as far as the facilities in ACs are concerned such as library (58.4%), laboratory(55.3%), and hostel facilities (53.9%). Colleges under the universities of Osmania, Bharathidasan, Bharathiar, and Madras seem to have better facilities. This is evident from the student responses; the reason could be that these colleges are pre-policy autonomous colleges, except the ones under the Osmania University. The scheme was implemented in these colleges in late 1970s and they have utilised the special grant received from the University Grants Commission to upgrade library, laboratory and hostel facilities.

TABLE V
TEACHERS PERFORMANCE IN AUTONOMOUS COLLEGE AS PERCEIVED BY STUDENTS

(In Percentages)

	Always come prepared to the class	Encourage questioning	Stimulate thinking	Provides up to date knowledge	Promote impartiality	Promotes punctuality	Take interest in students
Total (1021)	**79.6**	**74.3**	**68.9**	**67.2**	**65.8**	**74.2**	**70.2**
Managementwise							
Private (782)	62.3	56.3	52.3	50.1	49.5	57.3	52.3
Government (239)	17.3	18.0	16.6	17.1	16.3	16.9	17.9
Nature of College							
Men (96)	8.0	6.4	5.6	6.1	5.5	6.6	5.6
Women (222)	18.0	18.0	16.6	17.1	16.3	16.9	17.9
Co-edu.(703)	53.6	49.9	46.7	44.0	44.0	50.7	46.5
Autonomous Status							
Autonomous (895)	69.9	64.8	61.0	59.7	58.1	65.2	61.8
Non-Autonomous (126)	9.8	9.5	7.8	7.4	7.6	9.0	8.4
Statewise							
Andhra Pra. (317)	24.7	21.7	19.7	20.2	19.7	25.1	20.1
Tamil Nadu (317)	46.0	45.4	42.1	40.0	39.6	42.2	42.8
Rajasthan (13)	8.9	7.2	7.1	7.0	6.4	6.9	7.3
Universitywise							
Andhra (53)	3.4	3.7	3.2	2.9	3.9	4.2	3.0
Nagarjuna (59)	5.2	3.4	3.2	3.9	3.5	5.3	3.7
Osmania (175)	13.8	12.5	11.3	11.5	10.5	13.1	11.2
Bharathidasan(141)	11.0	11.3	10.8	9.0	10.0	9.5	10.3
Bharathiar (111)	10.4	9.3	8.8	8.0	7.4	10.1	8.3
Madras (224)	17.4	17.2	15.5	15.0	14.8	16.2	17.3
Madurai Kamaraj (37)	2.7	2.3	2.3	2.6	2.3	2.6	2.0
Ajmer (130)	8.9	7.2	7.1	7.0	6.5	6.9	7.3
S. Manomaniam (91)	6.8	7.4	6.7	7.3	6.9	6.3	7.1

Teacher Characteristics (Table VI)

Quality of education and promoting academic excellence is dependant upon teacher effectivenes. Items were introduced in the questionnaire to assess behavioural changes if any.

TABLE VI

JUSTIFICATION FOR CONTINUATION OF AUTONOMY AS PERCEIVED BY STUDENTS

(In Percentages)

	Autonomy Improves Standards education	Autonomy Fecilatates teaching & evaluation	Autonomy Promotes freedom	Autonomy Promotes better functi-oning college
Total (1021)	**79.9**	**76.3**	**66.0**	**72.5**
Managementwise				
Private (782)	66.8	63.2	53.4	60.2
Government (239)	13.1	13.1	12.6	12.3
Nature of College				
Men (96)	8.1	7.1	6.4	7.3
Women (222)	19.3	15.7	17.4	19.1
Co-educational (703)	52.5	53.5	42.2	46.1
Autonomous Status				
Autonomous (895)	70.0	67.3	59.3	64.3
Non-Autonomous (126)	9.6	9.1	6.9	8.2
Statewise				
Andhra Pradesh (317)	25.0	23.3	18.0	20.5
Tamil Nadu (574)	50.7	48.4	43.5	48.2
Rajasthan (130)	4.2	4.6	4.5	3.8
Universitywise				
Andhra (53)	4.6	4.2	2.6	3.7
Nagajuna (59)	5.6	4.8	3.5	4.6
Osmania (175)	14.8	14.3	1 1.9	12.2
Bharathidasan (141)	10.6	9.6	9.9	10.9
Bharthiar (111)	10.5	10.3	8.0	10.5
Madras (224)	19.5	19.2	15.5	17.3
Madurai Kamaraj (37)	2.6	2.8	2.5	2.0
Ajmer (130)	4.2	4.6	4.5	3.8
S. Manomaniam (91)	7.5	6.5	7.6	7.5

In teachers of ACs data reveals that performance of teachers in ACs is comparatively better than those of the affiliated colleges, if following are the indicators of teacher performance. i.e., teachers coming prepared to the class (79.6%), encourage questioning among students (74.3%), stimulates thinking (68.9%), provide up to date information (67.2%), promote impartiality (65.8%), promote punctuality (74.2%), and take interest in student activites (70.2%). The high percentage in support of the statement in favour of Autonomy. Further student-teacher relationships seems to be better in ACs in contrast to what is observed from the non-autonomous colleges. This might be due to the reason that the teachers feel and now that in the ACs if things go wrong, it is the teachers who are directly responsible as they are the ones who decide and implement all the academic matters of the college.

Continuation of Autonomy (Table VII)

The status of a college as autonomous is not conferred forever by the parent university. It is initially granted for a period of five years, and after completing five years, the committee constituted for the purpose will review its functioning and in fact autonomy will be extending only if it is found working satisfactorily. The Syndicate of the parent university is empowered to withdraw autonomy at any time it found unsatisfactory. In order to elicit the real feelings of the students towards the scheme, a question was asked about the continuance of the scheme in the college. Majority of the students viewed it in positive terms. The reasons given by the students for continuing autonomous scheme in the colleges is based on their experience under autonomy and whether it helps to improve the standards of education (79.9%), it facilitated in improving standards of teaching and evaluation (76.3%), it promoted academic freedom (66%) and it contributed to the better functioning of the college (72.5%).

Table VII

Administrative Style adopted by Principals and Teachers and existing inter personal relation in colleges as perceived by students (In percentages)

	Administrative Style						Interpersonal Relations		
	Principals			Teachers					
	Demo cratic	Lais-sez faire	Auto-cratic	Demo-cratic	Lias-sez faire	Auto-cratic	Stud.& Tea-chers	Stud.& Prin -cipal	Among stu-dents
Total	**59.5**	**14.8**	**12.8**	**53.2**	**18.6**	**11.4**	**31.7**	**39.1**	**31.9**
Manage-mentwise									
Private (782)	48.4	10.2	10.1	47.4	12.5	6.9	22.4	30.3	23.1
Govt. (239)	11.1	4.6	2.7	5.8	6.1	4.5	9.3	8.8	8.2
Nature of College									
Men (96)	5.3	1.1	1.5	4.8	1.7	.9	3.5	4.4	3.0
Women (222)	17.6	1.2	1.6	13.5	4.9	1.9	6.9	7.8	8.0
Co-educa tional (703)	36.5	12.3	9.6	35.0	11.7	8.2	21.3	26.9	20.1
Autonomous Status									
Autonomous College (895)	52.4	12.4	11.2	46.1	16.8	10.1	28.1	35.7	27.0
Non-Auto-nomous (126)	7.1	2.4	1.5	7.2	1.7	1.1	3.5	3.4	3.4
Statewise									
Andh.Pr.(317)	17.5	4.0	3.9	18.0	3.7	2.9	5.5	7.8	7.2
T. Nadu (574)	35.2	8.2	7.2	31.0	12.6	6.3	21.2	26.6	20.7
Raj. (130)	5.1	2.6	1.7	4.2	2.3	2.2	5.0	4.7	3.9
Univ.wise									
Andhra (53)	1.9	2.1	1.1	2.4	1.8	.7	1.1	1.9	1.2
Nagarjuna(59)	3.2	.5	1.2	3.6	.2	0.7	1.6	2.3	1.5
Osmania (175)	12.4	1.4	1.6	12.0	1.7	1.5	2.8	3.6	4.0
Bharathi dasan (141)	7.3	2.4	2.4	5.8	3.3	2.2	6.7	7.1	6.3
Bharathiar(111)	7.6	1.8	2.0	6.0	1.7	1.7	4.1	6.0	2.0
Madras (224)	13.3	2.8	2.4	12.6	4.1	1.6	6.0	8.7	6.6
M.Kamaraj(37)	2.2	.4	.1	2.4	.2	.1	.5	1.3	1.2
Ajmer (130)	5.1	2.6	1.7	7.2	2.3	2.2	5.0	4.7	3.8
S. Mano maniam (91)	7.4	.8	0	4.2	3.3	0.7	3.9	3.5	4.5

Regarding the justification for the continuation of the scheme, there is consistency among the responses. More than 65% responded in all categories, including government colleges, voted for continuation of autonomy to their colleges.

Style of Functioning (Table VIII)

The autonomous scheme envisaged decentralised administration to facilitate participation of teachers in decision making. Students responses reveal (59.5%) that the functioning in the ACs is democratic in style. Of course 14.8% did report *laisszes faire*, and 12.8% reported autocratic when it comes to Principal's style, whereas in the case of teachers, students responded that 53.2% followed democratic style, 18.6% *laisszes faire* and 11.4% autocratic style. Though the student's knowledge with regard to the style of functioning might not be authentic yet one cannot ignore the fact changes in the college atmosphere shall be felt by the students. This observation attains value because the sample included both UG and PG. Students and also students who have studied earlier in non-autonomous colleges.

TABLE VIII
TEACHERS SATISFACTION IN TERMS OF THEIR RELATIONSHIP WITH PRINCIPAL AND STUDENTS

(In Percentages)

Total (442)	**85.2**	Osmania (51)	10.1
Andhra Pradesh (105)	20.1	Bharathidasan (61)	12.7
Tamil Nadu	54.1	Bharathiar (45)	10.0
Rajasthan (83)	11.0	Madras (103)	22.1
Locationwise		Madurai Kamarai (22)	4.1
Urban (392)	7.56	S. Manomaniam (23)	5.2
Rural (50)	9.7	**Nature of College**	
Autonomous Status		Women (118)	25.4
Pre Policy (113)	25.1	Men (53)	14.5
Post Policy (329)	60.1	Co-educational (271)	45.3
Universitywise		**Managementwise**	
Andhra (27)	5.6	Private (267)	55.6
Nagarjuna (27)	4.3	Government (17)	29.6

Interpersonal Relations (Table IX)

The data gets support from another finding on interpersonal relationship. Students reported that there exists good interpersonal relationship between teachers and students (31.7%) between Principal and students (39.1%) and among students (31%) themselves.

Autonomy to college is also granted in the area of admissions. Colleges are supposed to evolve and introduce its own admission policy subject to the reservation policy of the government. It is generally alleged that freedom given to the colleges in determining policies of admission will be misused by the colleges for their advantage. The responses of the students who are the direct beneficiaries of the system reveal that students are satisfied (70.5%) with the admission procedure practiced in the college. (Table IX).

The response of students towards autonomous scheme explains that autonomy is viewed by the students community in positive direction. The sampled students feel that the positive benefits of the scheme are higher than the negative ones. Except in the state of Rajasthan, the implementation of the scheme is highly appreciated. The responses also include that of the non-autonomous colleges, students also feel that the systems is better than the one operating in the affiliating colleges.

The data has also highlighted that autonomy has created changes in the academic atmosphere of the colleges, facilitating and study discipline orientation among students. Similarly, appreciable changes are noticed in teaching methods, teacher effectiveness and evaluation methods. Further autonomy built hope among the students in the labour market. The overall response of the sampled students who are the real beneficiaries of the scheme support autonomy in these colleges.

TABLE IX
RESPONSES INDICATING SATISFACTION OF STUDENTS TOWARDS ADMISSION POLICY AND COURSE RELATED ISSUES

(In Percentages)

			Courses Offered		
	Admi-ssion Policy	Prospects of getting job	Good	Average	Need Based Courses
Total (l021)	**70.5**	**74.3**	**39.5**	**39.7**	**75.7**
Managementwise					
Private (782)	55.9	60.3	26.3	34.4	61.9
Goverment (239)	14.6	14.0	13.2	5.3	13.8
Nature of College					
Men (96)	6.9	7.0	3.9	2.9	6.8
Women (222)	16.6	17.0	7.9	10.7	18.2
Co-educational 03	47.2	50.3	27.7	26.1	50.7
Autonomous Status					
Autonomous (895)	62.0	65.0	33.9	35.0	66.2
Non-Autonomous(126)	8.6	9.4	5.6	4.6	9.4
Statewise					
Andhra Pradesh (31)	21.4	20.9	9.9	10.5	23.0
Tamil Nadu (574)	41.9	47.1	21.7	27.9	46.5
Raiasthan (l30)	7.2	6.3	7.9	1.3	6.2
Universitywise					
Andhra (53)	4.1	3.5	2.3	1.5	3.8
Nagarjuna (59)	5.1	4.7	1.4	2.1	4.7
Osmania (175)	12.2	12.7	6.2	6.9	14.5
Bharathidasan (l41)	9.3	10.3	5.5	6.3	10.7
Bharathiar (111)	7.6	8.3	3.6	4.7	9.4
Madras (224)	16.3	18.3	8.0	11.7	16.3
Madurai Kamaraj (37)	2.3	2.8	1.6	1.0	2.0
Ajmer (130)	7.2	6.3	7.9	1.3	6.2
S. Manomaniam (91)	6.4	7.4	3.0	4.2	8.1

Student's Feedback on Restructured Courses

Regarding the courses offered in ACs, the findings reveal (Table IX) that the colleges enjoy freedom as far as development of new courses is concerned. It is obvious that these colleges can keep in mind student' needs, local relevance, infrastructural facility and possiblility of getting it implemented. It is at the initiative of individual college and its faculty that can make the course attractive and relevant. Whereas in the affiliating system it is the university that determines the syllabus and curriculum to all its affiliated colleges which of course is uniform and colleges by themselves have no powers to change. Flexibility in the structure and in the implementation of the programmes visualised in scheme of autonomous colleges has been responsible for attracting good students and also successful implementation of the new courses. The item such as "whether ACs provide for some choices in combination of courses" 80.2% of the students expressed that ACs provide for more choices in the combination of courses to the extent, it has been able to provide for job-oriented courses (55.4%). The statewise Tamil Nadu and Andhra Pradesh and university-wise figures further support this finding except that of Ajmer University. 74.3% of the students believe that the courses that are started in ACs have good prospects of getting a job after completion. Some of the ACs has introduced courses that are not only job-oriented but also prepare more students for competitive examinations.

It is only 55.4% students feel that job-oriented courses have been introduced in ACs. 74.3% students feel that prospects of their getting job is higher in spite of the fact the complete restructuring is yet to take place in the ACs. Introduction of job-oriented courses are still in experimental stage. Yet 39.5% students are of the opinion that the course are good, and equal percentage i.e., 39.7% feel that it is average. No doubt, 75.7% feel that the course are need-based.

CHAPTER 14
ISSUES IN QUALITY ASSURANCE, ASSESSMENT AND ACCREDITATION IN HIGHER EDUCATION

*Madan Mohan Jha

Thinking of the Indian nation and its people and considering the premise that there are degeneration, deterioration and decline in standard and values in almost every sphere of life, one is inclined to recall that famous statement of Pandit Jawahar Lal Nehru, who, while delivering the convocation address in Allahabad University in 1947 had said, 'If the universities discharge their duties adequately, then, it is well with the nation and the people." Putting the statement in reverse, one is constrained to observe that, perhaps, the universities are not able to perform upto the expected level of excellence and standard. Suggestion, therefore, is that universities should lead the nation and the society rather than follow them. They should re-establish the norms and the standards for the country and the society to emulate.

2. The decline in the standard and quality of higher education in India has been a direct fall out of its massification since 1950's. With around 20 universities and 500 colleges on the eve of independence, the numbers have now increased to 237 universities and 9703 colleges. Nevertheless, the concern for 'determination of standard' had been felt by the Constitution makers even at that time so much so that a specific provision was incorporated in the schedule of the Constitution under the 'Union List' which kept the prime responsibility of "co-ordination and determination of standards in institutions for the higher education or research and scientific and techincal institutions" with the Government of India. The position has remained unchanged since then.

3. The Union Government created the first institutional mechanism for maintaining standard and quality in universities by establishing the University Grants Commission in 1956. The UGC has taken up several initiatives to secure quality in universities and colleges such as regulations

* Joint Secretary (Higher Education), H.R.D. Ministry, New Delhi

for the requirements of minimum infrastructure facilites, prescription of essential qualifications for the appointment of teachers, in-service orientation and training of teachers, and evaluation and assessment of performance of teachers. The most recent initiative in the area of quality assurance and assessment, on the part of the UGC, has been the setting up of the National Assessment and Accreditaiton Council (NAAC) in September, 1994 following the policy outline of the National Policy on Education, 1986 and the programme of action,1985 which observed, *inter-alia*, "Excellence in institutions of higher education is a function of many aspects, self-evaluation and self-improvement are important among them". A parallel body for the assessment and accreditation of the technical and management institutions has been established under the All India Council of Technical Education (AICTE) Act and has been named as the National Board of Accreditation (NBA). The NAAC and NBA are in the process of developing and standardizing the system of assessment and accreditation of institutions of higher learning and their programmes. While the universities and institutions have started, enthusiastically responding to the requests of these accrediting bodies and are offering themselves for the assessment and accreditation, a number of issues have started emerging in the fast developing scenario of higher education at the national and international level.

4. The *objective of this NOTE* is to flag some of such issues for discussion.

1. Institution Vs. Programme

Whether the emphasis should be on the review and evaluation of the entire academic institution, or instead, the individual academic programme or discipline should be the focus of quality assessment. There are experiences whereby within the same institution/university or college different disciplines or programme perform at a variance. Encouragement to programme review may give a stronger sense of pride and team spirit to the smaller groups of academicians who believe in taking challenges and excellence even under adverse circumstances. This will also provide stimulus for learning from within and build up pressure on the higher management body from the groups of teachers working for discipline or programme.

2. Process Vs. Product

It is not very easy to define the performance indicators while reviewing the processes that go into teaching and learning in educational institutions, that may vary from discipline to discipline, from region to region and from one group of learners to others, though some basic elements may remain common. The other view could be to concentrate on 'products', the results that a particular institution and programme provide for the individuals joining them and the society at large. Again the nature and quality of product may be difficult to define. It will all depend 'upon the institutions and programmes' mission statement which will have to be considered within the overall objectives and policies of the major stakeholders and that would involve the Government, in case of public institutions.

3. Balance between teaching, research and extension

Institutions of higher learning particularly universities and colleges in India are generally deemed to be centres for imparting for transferring information and knowledge to students by the process of teaching. There are some concerns for innovation, investigations and research but very little emphasis in extension and extra-mural studies though they are included in the statutes of most of the universities. The community looks forward to these insititutions not merely as the production centres for job seekers but as bodies that could investigate into the contemporary social and economic issues and find out solutions that are of immediate relevance to them. To some extent, all the three functions are interrelated also. A good teaching practice will emerge if there is a spirit of enquiry and learning in the milieu that may be provided by the operational area or region of the institutions. This leads to a departure from the I-Know-all mode of teaching and a shift from teaching-learning to learning-learning environment. The question is how much emphasis should be given to the various practices of teaching, aspects of research and extension work during the assessment? It will again depend upon the charter and mandate of the institutions concerned, but a national consensus requires to be built up so that the institutions of higher learning get an overall direction and they have a balanced growth to meet the need and aspirations of the people they are expected to serve.

4. *Emphasis on Self Study*

The current trend on quality assurance seems to be on the emphasis for the assessment and accreditation by the NAAC and the NBA, though the NAAC encourages the setting up of the Internal Quality Assurance Circle (IQAC) and asks for information and data and reporting by the self study groups of the institutions as a part of its assessment and accreditation process. The emphasis could shift to the self study evaluation by the institutions and units as a first step towards development proposals to be submitted to the UGC or other such funding agencies/government. The NAAC could help the institutions in the preparation of such proposals on the results of a self evaluation, according to explicit standards and expectations. The plans could be reviewed by the funding agencies, experts with attention to process and outcome. Successful institutions' would receive development grants to implement their proposals. Progress could be monitored on a regular basis and continued funding of the plan be based on the successful implementation of proposals. Such schemes have worked in the developing countries such as Indonesia with the support from the World Bank. The development grant related self-study would bring out the positive aspects of the quality assurance and would make the assessment and accreditation aspect of the NAAC/UGC less threatening and regulatory.

5. Educational Technology and Open Learning

The distinctions between the conventional university system of education where face-to-face contact is an essential feature for imparting knowledge and for distance education mode of learning where the learners may acquire knowledge even without coming to classroom and face-to-face contact with the teachers, are getting thinner and thinner, thanks to the rapid advancement of the educational and information technology and now the internet. Even the concept of distance education and open learning are changing very fast. Thus encouragement to life-long learning, retraining and further development of human skills and upgradation of knowledge would be the challenges of the 21st century that the university system would have to face if it wants to survive as the main centre and source of the evolution of knowledge society. Any system of quality assurance, assessement and accreditation would have to keep these aspects in view while evaluating the desire, capacity and potential of the institution and the units to respond to the new challenges of the demand and expectation from the higher institutions of learning.

6. Assessment and Accreditation of the Support System

Universities and colleges do not operate in vacuum. Their functions are supported by various institutional bodies. For instance, Academic Staff Colleges of the UGC train their teachers. There would be a need to develop a scheme for the accreditation of the teacher training programmes and the centres providing such training. Similarly, the assessment of other support system such as mechanism for funding, recruitment, procurement, testing etc., could also be assessed and accredited based on certain standard and healthy practices by competent expert bodies.

7. Whether Voluntary and Linkage with Funding

The debate on the question whether the accreditation should be voluntary or mandatory and whether funding should be linked with the levels of accreditation has already started. It is difficult to give a judgement at this point of time. It is understood while the NAAC encourages voluntary assessment and the accreditation of technical and management institutions by the NBA/AICTE is rather mandatory. It will all depend upon the creditability of the accrediting agencies and acceptability of the system and process developed by them. If they are able to raise the confidence of the institutions as also of the students, parents and funding agencies there is no reason why the institutions would not like to join the quality march, get assessed and strive for further improvement that could be linked with the funding support and self resource generation, leading to turning institutions into centres of excellence.

8. Why NAAC/NBA ONLY?

The question is whether we should have only government supported accrediting agencies for various sectors of education or multiple agencies may be allowed to grow. Why cannot the assessment and accrediting activities be taken up in the NGO sector? The competition among various accrediting agencies may improve the quality and acceptability of the assessment itself. This will provide options to the institutions and also a chance to students and parents to judge the agencies. The transparency combined with the public reporting will reduce for elements of doubt on processes and procedures.

9. *International Academic Mobility*

International mobility of students, teachers and researchers are another areas that would require a close attention by the promoters and protectors of quality in higher education in the coming century. Trade and economics have already reduced the width of the inter-nation boundaries and education, particularly higher education and electronic learning is going to diminish it further. Strength of the institutions to attract foreign students particularly Indian students and teachers abroad would be an interesting area of enquiry and would be directly related to the quality and nature of education and programme being offered by them. The question of brain drain will have to be addressed in its totality and advantages to the institutions and the country as a whole will have to be assessed with the export of Indian scholars on a long term basis.

Conclusion

10. These are some of the challenges of quality parameters that perhaps need to be addressed. The national quality assurance agencies may consider ways in which they would be able to contribute to the development of newer models for quality evaluation and assessment whereby focus is on learning rather than on the setting in which learning takes place; emphasis is on users' and accepters' satisfaction rather than providers' need and expectations and the thrust is on making the universities discharging their duties well rather than waiting for the nation and the people to take initiative and the lead.

Chapter 15
Autonomous Colleges and International Accreditation

Dr. B. Sampath Kumar*

"Nothing is more advantageous and more creditable than a rich heritage. But nothing is more dangerous for a nation than to sit back and live on that heritage. A nation cannot progress if it merely imitates its ancestors. What builds a nation is creative, inventive and vital activity."

Pandit Jawaharlal Nehru

SINCE Independence there had always been a demand to revamp the educational system in India. Although various endeavours have been made both by the Central and State Governments in this direction in the past fifty years of Independence, we have yet to go a long way to educate the masses. With a view to reorient and reform the educational system a number of committees at the National and the State level had been constituted which recommended a number of solutions to change the educational system.

After the Gurukula system of education a new system was introduced by the western rulers in which the teachers and taught assembled in a common place and the teachers imparted knowledge to the taught. This system of education enabled all the citizens of our nation to get education. At all levels of education, right from the elementary to college levels this system is being followed scrupulously. Though the system is the same, the administration varies with variations in the level of education. In this, the institutions of higher education are affiliated to universities. The parent universities act as the supreme body on all academic matters developing the curricula, preparing the syllabus, conducting the examinations, publishing the results and awarding the degrees to the successful candidates. The colleges used to get the guidance and advice on all academic matters from the university. This system was effective when the number of affiliated colleges was less

Principal, PSG Arts and Science College, Coimbatore

and number of courses were also limited. Due to an enormous increase in the number of colleges, in the courses offered and in the number of students opting for higher education, a new system in lieu of affiliating system had to be brought in.

Further, the academic decisions also had to be made, according to the changing needs of the society, keeping pace with the ever-changing demands of the society and in preparing the need-based curriculum and syllabus. These were found difficult in the affiliating system, due to the large number of affiliated collegs in the university, which became a drag on the process of modernization and improvement of standards.

In the affilliating system, the colleges that had the potentiality to have higher standard of education did not have the freedom to develop the need-based curriculum and syllabus. It was felt that the innovations could be speedily introduced and implemented effectively in a smaller body. Keeping all these factors in mind the UGC introduced "autonomy" to colleges which had the potential to undertake innovations, design need-based curricula and syllabus, evolve method of teaching and learning and conduct the examination. In the year 1978, the first batch of five colleges in Tamil Nadu was conferred autonomy. Now as many as 48 colleges enjoy the autonomous status in Tamil Nadu. The University Grants Commission issues guidelines to regulate the functioning of the autonomous collegs.

The autonomous colleges have the freedom to determine and prescribe their own curriculum and syllabus, evolve methods of evaluation and to conduct examination. However, the parent university reserves the right to confer the degree on the successful students from autonomous colleges. The autonomous colleges now have their own system of education. The system, even though specific, has some commonality with regard to administration, designing of the course, preparation of the syllabus, methods of teaching, components of evaluation and pattern of examination.

Administration in Autonomous Colleges

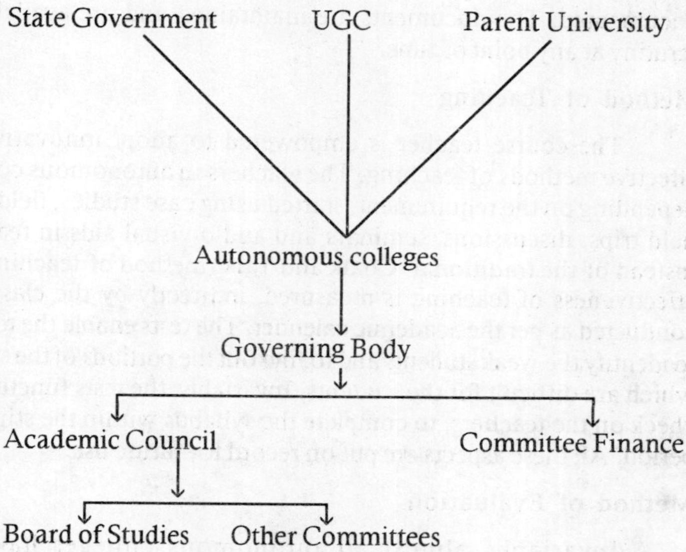

The other Committees are Planning and Evaluation Committee, Grievances and Appeals Committee, Examination Committee, Admission Committee, Library Committee and Students' welfare and extra-curricular Committee.

In all committees there are representatives of the UGC, State Govt., parent university, subject experts and teachers, as per the UGC guidelines. The functioning of the committees is highly systemised in all autonomous colleges.

Couses and Syllabus

The autonomous colleges prepare the need-based courses and syllabus to suit the local conditions and demand. The innovative courses introduced by the autonomous colleges are well received by the students, since the courses are employment oriented. Moreover, the autonomous colleges change the curricula and syllabi at frequent intervals to meet the demands in the employment market. The Autonomy has enabled the colleges to introduce vocational subjects, self-study papers and invisible component like Personality Development, Yoga, Computer courses, Food Preservation and the like in the course content.

The whole process of preparation of the course content and syllabus is carried out by the respective department, finalised by the Board of Studies, approved by the Academic Council and is properly documented. The documents are maintained and are available for scrutiny at any point of time.

Method of Teaching

The course teacher is empowered to adopt innovative and effective methods of teaching. The teachers in autonomous colleges, depending on the requirement, started using case studies, field work, field trips, discussions, seminars and audio-visual aids in teaching, instead of the traditional "Chalk and Talk" method of teaching. The effectiveness of teaching is measured, indirectly by the class tests, conducted as per the academic calender. The tests enable the teachers to identify the weak students and to find out the portions of the syllabus which are difficult for the students. Invariably, the tests function as a check on the teachers, to complete the syllabus within the stipulated period. All these aspects are put on record for future use.

Method of Evaluation

Invariably, almost all-autonomous colleges have two components in evaluating the students. The first component is the continuous assessment (CA) and the second is the end semester examination (ESE).

The ratio between CA and ESE varies from college to college. The components for CA also vary. Some colleges have two valuations for UG and PG and some other colleges have two valuations only for PG courses. In case the difference in marks between two valuations is more than 15% the script is sent for third valuation.

The question papers for ESE are normally set by the internal as well as external examiners. In practice, the Board of Studies prepares the list of teachers for paper setting and for valuation. From the list, the Controller of Examinations selects the teachers for the confidential work. However, the tests, quiz, etc. are conducted by the course teachers and marks are awarded. The system is highly confidential and secrecy is maintained at all levels. The review commitees appointed by the Parent Universities and by UGC complimented the system followed in the autonomous colleges and were satisfied with the documents maintained in the colleges.

The autonomous colleges encourage the participation of teachers and students at all levels of development. Special provisions are made by the UGC for the teachers to attend seminars, conferences, refresher courses and to do research to update their subject knowledge. The college teachers can express their opinion on the academic matters in various forums. The students also have the freedom to air their grievances pertaining to the examination, infrastructural facilities and welfare measures. All the activities of the autonomous colleges are 'student centred' i.e., consumer centred.

All these aspects of autonomy created an effective system of functioning of the colleges. In this system, there is planning, there is effective implementation, there is periodic evaluation, there is a feedback and there is provision for re-structuring of courses to meet the consumer's demands. Because of the effective and fool-proof system, the autonomous colleges are better recognized in the academic world and preferred by the students, parents and by the society to the affiliated colleges.

Further, the working of autonomous colleges normally is not affected by the general disturbances. The students unrest is also very minimum. In other words, the academic environment is better in autonomous colleges than in affiliated colleges.

Above all, the autonomous colleges have the privilege of applying for the accreditation to the National Assessment and Accreditation Council sponsored by UGC. But the Council sanctioned accreditation to the courses and syllabus and not to the system as such. This accreditation is at the national level and most of the autonomous colleges, were already accredited by the council or are in the process of getting accreditation. At this juncture there are a few pertinent questions. Is it not time to get international recognition to autonomous colleges? Are we to remain satisfied just with their autonomious status alone?

Another important aspects to be noted here is that the foreign universities started thinking of having an understanding with the Indian universities for faculty exchange and for student exchange programmes. At this juncture it would be better if the autonomous colleges had international accreditation.

Here an attempt is made to fit our system in the international standard to which the guidelines are given by the International Standard Organization (ISO)*. Before making an attempt to fit the system being

* ISO is now called as International Organization for Standardization

followed in autonomous colleges to the ISO guidelines, it becomes pertinent to give a brief note on ISO 9004.2 which gives the guidelines for service industries.

"ISO"

The International Standard Organization (ISO) brought out a set of standards pertaining to not only the quality of the products but to the practice of quality assurance system within the institution (ISO 9000) as well. It was originally issued as a series of six internationally agreed upon standards to guide and audit an institution, quality management practices, documents and records. Each standard contains specific guidelines pertaining to certain segments of quality related activities. Each provides the basic framework for an organization to install quality management practices and to follow sound and comprehensive quality concept, definition of term requirements and guidelines. The standards are the minmum acceptable level of standards that an institution's quality management practices should meet. ISO 9000 is neither mandatory nor a government regulation.

ISO 9004.2 gives broad guidelines that are applied in service sector which includes Hospitals, Trading, Finance, Education and the like.

It gives guidance for establishing and implementing a quality system within a institution. It can be applied directly when implementing a quality system for an existing service. The quality system embraces all the processes needed to provide an effective service and includes analysis of service provided to customers.

In a quality system, the customer is the focal point of the three key aspects viz., Management Responsibility (MR), Quality System Structure (QSS), and Personnel and Material Resources (PMR).

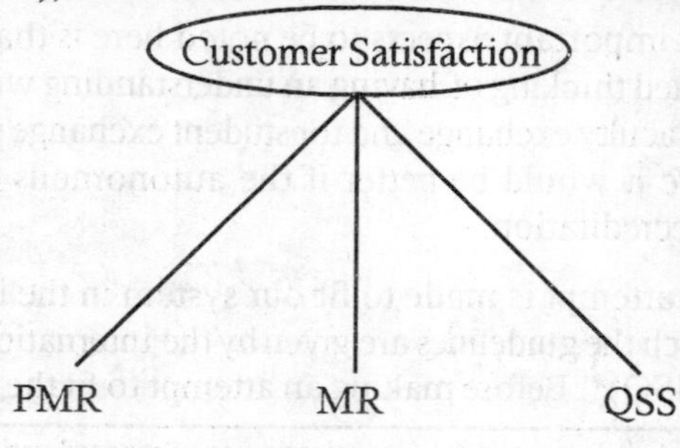

Management Responsibility (MR)

The Management is responsible for establishing a policy for the service quality and customer satisfaction. The successful implementation of this policy depends upon managements' commitment to the development and effective operation of a quality system.

The management should develop and document a quality policy relating to

1. Grade of service to be provided
2. Organization's image and reputation for quality
3. Objectives for service quality
4. Approach to be adopted in pursuit of quality objectives and
5. Role of institution's personnel responsible for implementing the quality policy.

The management should develop and document a quality policy that is promulgated, understood, implemented and maintained.

The quality objective includes customer satisfaction, continuous improvement to meet the requirement of the society and efficient control, evaluation and improvement of service quality throughout all the stages of the provision of a service. The responsibility and authority should be clearly defined for all personnel whose activities influence service quality. The management can have a management representative who is responsible for ensuring the quality system that is established, audited, continuously measured and reviewed for improvement.

While personnel with specific designated responsibilities can be instrumental in the attainment of quality, it should be stressed that it is not these representatives who create quality. They are only part of the quality system. The people of the quality system encompass all the functionaries and require the involvement, commitment and effective inter-working of all personnel in the organization to achieve continuous improvement.

Management should provide for formal periodic and independent reviews of the quality policy and achieving the quality objectives. The review should be carried out by appropriate, competent and independent personnel and it should consist of well-structured and comprehensive evaluation encompassing all relevant sources of information.

Personnel and Material Resouces (PMR)

A most important resource in any organization is securing personnel involvement. The behaviour and performence of individuals have direct impact on the quality of service. The management should appoint the personnel who are capable, creative and consistent to meet the job specification,who can secure and influence the work relationship, contribute and enhance the quality of service, who have involvement, commitment and better understanding of the work environment. The management has the responsibility to train and develop the personnel.

The material resources include the equipment, stores, accommodation, information system, quality assessment facilities, computer software and operational and technical documentation.

Quality System Structure (QSS)

The service organization should develop, establish, document, implement and maintain a quality system as a means by which stated policies and objectives for service quality may be accomplished. The element of quality should be structured to establish adequate control and assurance of overall operational processes affecting service quality.

All service element requirements and provisions incorporated in the quality system should be defined and documented. Appropriate quality system documentation includes quality manual, documentation control (approved by the authorized persons, easily understandable and acceptable to users, revised as and when required.)

Internal audits should be performed periodically to verify the implementation and effectiveness of the quality system and adherence to the service specification. It should be planned and recorded in accordance with the documental procedures framed by the competent authority. Audit findings should be submitted to the higher authority who would initiate necessary and appropriate corrective actions. The implementation and effectiveness of the corrective actions should also be assured.

The management should establish effective interaction between the organization and the customer.

Autonomous Colleges and ISO 9004.2

In the forthcoming part of the paper the guidelines given in ISO 9004.2 are discussed in relation to the system being followed in the autonomous colleges.

The general objective of ISO is consumer satisfaction. Here in autonomous colleges the consumers are the students, the parents and the society. All the three groups are satisfied with the educational standards maintained in the autonomous colleges. The satisfaction is mainly because of the need based syllabus, frequent review and revising of syllabus to suit the needs and the demands of the society, employment oriented curriculum with special courses, early publication of results which helps the students to get employment or to pursue higher studies immediatey after their college education, and continuous assessment system which keeps the students busy academically throughout the year.

The other components are quality policy, management responsibility, quality system structure and personnel annd material resources.

The autonomous colleges committed to develop a standard of education have a clearcut well-defined quality policy. The policy is formed based on the guidelines issued by the UGC from to time, by the competent authority and followed *in toto*. As such, the quality policy in autonomous colleges includes the policy on the formation of the various committees, mode of their functioning, their role, responsibilities and authority, the policy on the designing of the courses and syllabus, the policy on teacher development programmes, the policy on evaluation and method of examination and the like.

The management of the autonomous college is committed for the development of education, continuous improvement of education, and effective operation of the quality policy. It has the responsibility for the improvement of quality education through the improvement of teachers, and the enhancement of infrastructural facilities.

The quality structure is also followed in the autonomous colleges. The system structure in the colleges has the documentation system stating the quality to be maintained in the college, organizational structure of the college; viz. Governing Counsil, Academic Council, Board of Studies, Finance Committee (with responsibility and power) has specific procedures for framing, designing courses and syllabus for conducting the examination and method of evaluation and for the feedback. The process is recorded and kept for the future use. The review committees scrutinize such documents periodically and vouch for the validity.

With the financial assistance from the apex body the colleges motivate the teachers to attend courses to update themselves and to do research in areas of interest and to take up any other development programmes.

Further the institutional development is possible only when the personnel in the institution are developed, in accordance with the development policies of the organization. The concept of 'Human Resources Development' may be given due importance in the educational institutions. The autonomous colleges are already encouraging the teachers to develop themselves academically.

In addition, the required infrastructural facilities like library, laboratory for providing information, and others for extracurricular activities are better provided in the autonomous college than in the affiliated colleges.

To sum up, autonomous colleges have well-developed system to impart quality education to the younger generation to the satisfaction of the society. But the colleges still do not get the international recognition, which the colleges very well deserve. The colleges already have the required standard to do service. Hence now an earnest attempt should be made to get the international accreditation which is the only means of achieving Total Quality Management in educational institutions. Moreover, the 'Globalization in Education' is possible, if the autonomous colleges obtained "international accreditation".